"Therefore encourage one another and build each other up, just as in fact you are doing."

—1 Thessalonians 5:11 (NIV)

WHISTLE STOP
Café
MYSTERIES

# ACCENTUATE the POSITIVE

## JEANETTE HANSCOME

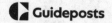

Guideposts

Whistle Stop Café Mysteries is a trademark of Guideposts.

Published by Guideposts
100 Reserve Road, Suite E200
Danbury, CT 06810
Guideposts.org

This is a work of fiction. While the setting of Whistle Stop Café Mysteries as presented in this series is fictional, the location of Dennison, Ohio, actually exists, and some places and characters may be based on actual places and people whose identities have been used with permission or fictionalized to protect their privacy. Apart from the actual people, events, and locales that figure into the fiction narrative, all other names, characters, businesses, and events are the creation of the author's imagination and any resemblance to actual persons or events is coincidental.

Every attempt has been made to credit the sources of copyrighted material used in this book. If any such acknowledgment has been inadvertently omitted or miscredited, receipt of such information would be appreciated.

Scripture references are from the following sources: *The Holy Bible, King James Version* (KJV). *The Holy Bible, New International Version* (NIV). Copyright © 1973, 1978, 1984, 2011 by Biblica, Inc. Used by permission of Zondervan. All rights reserved worldwide. www.zondervan.com

Cover and interior design by Müllerhaus
Cover illustration by Greg Copeland at Illustration Online LLC.
Typeset by Aptara, Inc.

ISBN 978-1-961126-02-2 (hardcover)
ISBN 978-1-961126-03-9 (epub)

Printed and bound in the United States of America
10 9 8 7 6 5 4 3 2 1

# ACCENTUATE
# the POSITIVE

# CHAPTER ONE

*J*anet Shaw unzipped her coat in the homey warmth of Aunt Maggie's Antiques and Consignment. Getting there had required her husband, Ian, to drive only a few miles outside Dennison, but on this first Sunday after putting away everything holiday related, it felt like an exciting post-Christmas road trip.

She took a business card from the welcome table near the door of what had once been a Victorian house. "Debbie will love this place," she said to Ian. "Too bad we didn't know about it during the holidays. I bet it was adorable."

Janet had stumbled upon Aunt Maggie's online while helping her daughter Tiffany search for an affordable pair of boots for a spur-of-the-moment ski trip. It looked even better than in the pictures. A fire burned in a woodstove in the corner. A few feet away, a round table covered with a royal-blue tablecloth welcomed customers with a plate of cookies and thermoses marked *hot apple cider* and *coffee*.

Janet took her husband's hand. "Thanks for getting me out today."

Ian gave her hand a gentle squeeze. "The house felt too quiet to me too."

Janet examined the contents of a square glass case near the cookie table. It held more expensive antique jewelry and watches.

"I guess it's the price we pay for having a daughter who knows how to make friends."

Tiffany would still be at home on winter break if not for a call from her college roommate, who'd invited her to take a sick friend's place on the ski trip. "At least she's having fun before second-semester classes start."

A slender middle-aged woman sitting behind the cash register put aside her kitting. "Is there anything special you're looking for?"

Janet picked up a rose-printed teacup to admire the pattern. "Just browsing. Are you Aunt Maggie?"

"No. Maggie was my aunt. My great-aunt, technically. My husband and I bought this house from her family after she passed away. I'm Anne."

Ian helped himself to a cup of cider. "You have a nice place here."

"Thank you."

Enticed by the sweet aroma of Ian's cider, Janet poured herself some as well. "How long have you been open?"

"Just since June." Anne walked around to the front of the white cashier counter adorned with baskets of impulse buys. "You're one of the women who runs the Whistle Stop Café at the Dennison train station, aren't you?"

"Sure am. I'm Janet."

"My husband and I were there a few days before Christmas. I had some of your yummy gingerbread."

Janet made a mental note to make more gingerbread for the upcoming week. She wrapped her hands around the steaming cup of cider and breathed in the cinnamon-clove-infused goodness. "I hope you come back again."

"I'm sure I will." Anne returned to her chair and picked up her knitting. "Feel free to look around as long as you like."

Janet sipped her cider and ventured over to one of the side rooms while Ian thumbed through a trunk of old *Life* magazines.

The small room was set up like a den, with old books for sale on built-in shelves, tables of stationery and handmade journals, a cozy chair draped with throws, and a rolltop desk.

A portable lap desk with swirly carving along the edges sat smack-dab in the middle of the open rolltop. It called to Janet. The lap desk even had two narrow drawers in front and a hole for an ink bottle.

Ian came in as she was searching for a price tag.

Janet reached for one of the drawers then noticed the *Please don't touch. Ask for assistance* card on top. "My grandmother had a portable desk similar to this one. She used it for writing letters and cards for birthdays and holidays." She could still hear the *scritch scritch* of Grammy's Parker fountain pen, her favorite tool for letter writing.

Ian finished off his cider and tossed his cup in a wastebasket beside the rolltop desk. "Did you see how much it costs?"

Janet shook her head and turned around to call for Anne. But Anne was already on her way over.

"I just set that out yesterday," she said. "I found it while I was putting away holiday decorations. I'm sure it belonged to someone in Aunt Maggie's family. I thought about keeping it, but if I held on to every lovely item I found among her things, our house would look like—" She waved one hand at the desk and the other toward a table stacked with vintage-style calendars. "Well, like this store. Cute, but no place to sit."

Janet put her hands behind her back to keep herself from breaking the *Please don't touch* rule. "Did you find anything interesting inside it?"

Anne's big brown eyes grew wide and bright. "It was a gold mine of old stationery and postcards." She lifted the lid that doubled as a writing surface, uncovering neat stacks of cards, paper, and envelopes. "I also found some photos and an old composition book with a lot of writing in it. Those I kept. But everything that was unused, I decided to include with the desk." Anne stepped aside. "You can touch it. I added the sign so kids wouldn't mistake it for an art station and make a mess."

Janet relaxed and opened one of the drawers. It contained a pack of multicolored gel pens and a small box of ballpoints. "I can see why kids might mistake this for an art station."

"I didn't want to offer all that stationery without something to write with." Anne picked up a small rectangular box beside the lap desk. "Look at this fun little treasure." She opened the box and took out a copper-colored pen. When she held it up to the light, a unique marble effect contrasted the copper. She unscrewed the cap. "It's a fountain pen."

Ian touched the barrel. "That's a unique color."

"Isn't it great? It works really well. I filled it with fresh ink and tried it out."

Janet took the pen from Anne to get a closer look. The *Parker* stamp on the clip immediately triggered a memory of her grandmother. Grammy's pen had been red. "You found this in the lap desk?" The gold nib was stamped with *Parker Duofold*, as was the side of the pen, so it wasn't exactly like Grammy's. But similar enough.

"I almost included it with the other pens, but I knew my husband would insist I sell it separately, so I found a box for it."

Janet set the pen back in the box and found a price on the side. Fifteen dollars.

Anne positioned the box in a way that caused the overhead light to shine on a partially rubbed off *M* in the *Made in USA* stamp. "I had to guess on the price until my husband returns from visiting his mom. He's the pen person. My specialty is china and old furniture."

Ian opened another drawer in the desk that contained more note cards. "Whoever owned this desk and pen really liked to write."

Janet went back to admiring the desk. She imagined it in the café, along with the copper fountain pen. "I wonder what Debbie would think of displaying these in the café. I know they aren't train-related, but—"

"You should go ahead and get them." Ian picked up the fountain pen. He took an old receipt out of his pocket and printed his name. "If Debbie doesn't think they're a good match for the café, we'll find a place for the desk at home, and you can use the fountain pen to write recipes the old-fashioned way." He handed it to Janet.

Janet poised it in the writing position. "That would be fun."

"You know what?" Anne shut the desk and pulled a price sticker off the back of it. "If you want both for the café, I'll knock off ten percent and throw in the bottle of refill ink I bought for the fountain pen."

Janet looked up at Ian and nodded.

"It's a deal," he said.

Anne smiled and picked up the little writing desk and the box containing the pen. "It won't hurt my feelings if you decide to toss the old stationery and use the other pens at the café. I just wanted the desk to look complete."

At the register, Janet ran her hands over the smooth wood of the desk and the intricate etchings along the sides, again hearing the scritch of her grandma writing letters to friends while her grandchildren played or watched television. She still had a few of the cards she'd received from Grammy—special ones that included notes that she treasured. She opened the lid, tucked the boxed fountain pen between the stacks of cards and envelopes, and said, "I think I know exactly what I want to do with the stationery."

The next morning, Janet slipped a red-and-white polka-dot apron over the I'M KIND OF A BIG DEAL sweatshirt that Tiffany had given her for Christmas. She went over to the lap desk that she'd placed on a rustic square table near the entrance of the café. The smell of fresh cinnamon rolls and gingerbread added an extra sense of comfort on a cold Monday morning.

Debbie Albright walked into the dining area from the kitchen. "I'm so glad Ian talked you into getting that. Thanks for sharing it with the café."

Janet reached behind the table and pulled out the part of the display she hadn't shared with Debbie yet. "I'm glad you like it. Because I have an idea." She held up a corkboard that had once hung in Tiffany's room covered with pictures of friends, favorite actors, school certificates, and postcards from family trips. "I think it'll be fun for customers, and even for us." She stood back to give Debbie room to fully take in her creation.

MAKE SOMEONE'S DAY IN THE DREARY MONTH OF JANUARY!
WRITE AN ENCOURAGING WORD, QUOTE, OR VERSE.
TACK IT TO THE BOARD FOR OTHERS TO ENJOY.
BE CREATIVE. ALL WE ASK IS THAT YOU KEEP IT CLEAN
AND UPLIFTING.

"This is great." Debbie took the board from her. She set it behind the desk and leaned it against the wall. "There. Now customers can start using it. We can hang it on the wall later to make it more secure."

Janet pushed a chair up to the table. "I cut the sheets of stationery in halves and fourths." She opened the drawer that Anne had filled with pens. "If customers don't go for it, we can post encouraging notes of our own." She opened both packs of pens, selected a few from each, and dropped them into the hole that would have held an ink bottle back in the day. She retrieved a container of tacks from another drawer and set it beside the desk. Then she opened the desk to reveal the pièce de résistance—the wooden box containing her gorgeous fountain pen. She lifted the lid with a flourish. "Ta-da! I wrote a card to my parents with it last night to try it out. It was so fun."

"Are you sure you want to put that out? It looks pretty fancy."

"Sure I'm sure. What's the fun of having a pretty pen if it never gets used?"

"True enough." Debbie flipped the Closed sign to Open. "I'll bring a quote book from home tomorrow in case people need some inspiration and want to copy one."

Janet found her phone and took a picture of the new writing station and the pen. She reached into her tote bag for the little sign she'd made.

PLEASE BE CAREFUL WHEN USING THE FOUNTAIN PEN.

Debbie slipped an order pad into the pocket of her apron. "This will be a perfect winter activity."

Janet peeked through the window to check for their first customer but didn't see anyone yet. She removed the cap from the fountain pen and took out a note card. "I'll get us started."

She took a seat in the chair to write. The satisfying scratch of the pen's nib against the wood of the lap desk made her a little giddy inside, even though her penmanship wasn't nearly as lovely as Grammy's used to be. She took a tack out of the cup and stuck her note to the corkboard.

*Give yourself a great day!*

***

Patricia Franklin was the first regular to show up at the café. She rubbed her gloved hands together. "Whew, it is nippy out there."

Janet took her place behind the bakery case. "What are you in the mood for today besides your usual peppermint mocha? I have some cinnamon rolls straight from the oven, along with apple-spice muffins and the gingerbread that has been such a hit lately…"

Patricia rested her chin on her fingers and peered into the case. "Hmm. I've been hearing good things about your gingerbread."

"Gingerbread it is. Would you like some whipped cream on it?"

"Why not?"

Janet chatted with Patricia while plating her cake and preparing her mocha. "Do you have a busy day ahead of you?"

Patricia settled herself on a stool at the counter. The dramatic thud of her overstuffed tote bag hitting the stool beside her said it all. "The law profession doesn't stop for winter, that's for sure."

Janet sprayed an extra-large swirl of whipped cream on top of Patricia's cake and dusted her mocha with cocoa powder. "There you go. A little extra sweetness to get you going this morning."

Patricia licked her lips. "This is really good. I should appear stressed more often." She looked around the empty dining area. Janet knew Patricia noticed the writing station when she said, "Aw. That note on your new board just made my morning."

Janet handed her a napkin. "Exactly what I was hoping for."

As Patricia savored her first bite of gingerbread, Janet spotted Harry Franklin and his friendly dog, Crosby, right outside the café, in the part of the depot that used to serve as an indoor waiting area.

As soon as Harry opened the door to come in, Crosby gave himself a shake, sending snow flying off his red tartan dog sweater and grayish-white coat. Harry pointed to the writing desk. "I like your new accessory." He went over for a closer look and picked up the fountain pen. "I used to have one of these." He waved to his granddaughter and returned the pen to its box. "Morning, Patricia."

Patricia wiped her lips with a napkin. "Morning, Pop Pop."

A white-haired woman Janet had never seen before came in behind Harry. It was hard to guess her age. With her posture, stylish purse, and colorful scarf, Janet guessed that she was one of those women who'd learned how to appear younger than she really was. She stopped to examine the writing desk and picked up the fountain pen before asking to be seated near the window. Harry gave her a friendly nod as Debbie escorted her to a table.

Janet took a mug off the tray behind her. "What can I get for you, Harry?"

He eyed Patricia's drink. "I'll take one of those peppermint mochas. You only live once."

Patricia raised her cup. "Amen." She reached down to pet Crosby. "Hey, boy. Don't you look handsome?"

Harry took a seat beside Patricia at the counter. "Can I get it in a to-go cup? I have a class this morning."

Janet started Harry's mocha. "That's so cool. Did you sign up for one of those art classes at the community center?" One of the things Janet loved most about Harry was his ability to enjoy a full life despite being in his midnineties.

"No, a nice lady named Kate Lipton is offering a free writing workshop every Monday and Wednesday morning for the next four weeks to help us old-timers tell our life stories. It meets at Good Shepherd, but all seniors in the community are welcome. Since I qualify, I thought I'd try it out."

Janet forced herself not to react to Harry's words. She hadn't heard the name Kate Lipton since Debbie lived in Cleveland and shared frequent stories about a woman by that name who attended the same church she did. Debbie's Kate Lipton ran a window and glass business with her husband and managed to be in charge of everything from Bible studies to the women's ministries newsletter. Could Harry be talking about a different Kate Lipton? Based on what she remembered about Debbie's old church acquaintance, Dennison wasn't her scene at all.

Debbie handed Janet the older woman's order for an apple-spice muffin and hot tea. As she did, she shot Janet a confused look. Janet guessed Debbie was thinking the same thing about the person Harry had called Kate Lipton.

Patricia stabbed her fork into her slice of gingerbread. "I'm proud of you, Pop Pop."

"So am I," the woman seated by the window said. "Never stop learning. That's my motto."

"See." Janet took a to-go cup off the stack beside the espresso maker. "Even first-time customers are impressed."

Debbie set a mug and a basket of tea bags in front of the woman by the window. "Let me know if you'd like more hot water."

Harry rubbed the top of Crosby's head and turned to face the newcomer. "I'm sure you can still sign up if you're interested. I didn't see anything about the workshop being full."

The corners of the woman's lips curved upward. She raised her eyebrow and picked up her mug. "Maybe I'll pop in sometime."

Janet handed the woman's muffin to Debbie then delivered Harry's to-go mocha. "You're an inspiration to us all, Harry Franklin."

"I don't know about that." Harry turned his face away, but not before Janet noticed his grin. "But I do think it'll be interesting to hear everyone's stories. Eileen and Ray signed up too. Who knows, we might learn some new things about each other."

The woman by the window broke her muffin in half. She alternated her attention between the writing desk and Harry.

Harry checked his watch. "Well, I better say goodbye. Class starts at ten sharp, and I still need to stop by the drugstore to buy a notebook. I don't want to be tardy." He reached into his pocket and pulled out his wallet.

Patricia held up her hand. "Put your money away. This one's on me. You used to buy me first-day-of-school treats. Now it's my turn."

Harry gave Patricia a peck on the cheek. "Why, thank you." He pointed his paper cup at the writing desk. "I look forward to adding something to the message board when I can think of a profound statement. Now that I'm a writer and all." He gripped Crosby's leash and led him to the door. "Come on, boy. Let's go tell some stories."

Janet ran a damp cloth over the milk frother so it would be clean for the next mocha or latte order. "Have fun, Harry. Oh, and if that fountain pen reminds you of one you once had, I'll let you borrow it to write one of your stories with it for old time's sake."

Harry took another look at the pen. "I think I will."

The woman by the window waved to Harry, and he waved back. A trickle of customers eager for morning coffee prevented Janet from going over to introduce herself. Paulette arrived just in time to help with the rush. By the time Janet had said goodbye to Patricia, served pastries and fancy coffees, and replenished the popular gingerbread, the woman had left. Enough cash to cover her tea, muffin, and a generous tip lay on the table under the sugar bowl. Janet handed the bills to Debbie. "I hope she comes back. She seemed like a nice woman."

Debbie took the money to the cash register. "And very interested in Harry."

Janet smiled. "It did look like she was watching him." She walked over to the writing station to see if anyone had left a note. Patricia had added one in blue gel pen.

*The Whistle Stop Café is heaven on earth with extra sweetness.*

She spotted another note in the middle of the board. "Debbie, you have to see this." She pointed to the cream-colored card with the perfect fountain-pen handwriting. "Look. It's for Harry."

# CHAPTER TWO

*December 30, 1944*

*Harry Franklin adjusted his porter's cap and added the last piece of luggage to the baggage car. The snow had taken a break from falling just long enough for passengers to enjoy the fifteen-minute noon stop at Dennison Station.*

*Eileen Turner walked along the tracks with an overcoat covering her stationmaster's uniform. "The eastbound train will board in five minutes, folks."*

*Harry looked around for any remaining bags and watched clusters of servicemen make use of their final moments before either getting back on the train or boarding for the first time. Those who didn't have family or a girlfriend seeing them off were getting last-minute sandwiches, cookies, fruit, cups of coffee, magazines, and newspapers from the Salvation Army* canteen, all free of charge. Harry never got tired of watching them receive a little taste of home from the many volunteers who served with smiles and warm expressions of gratitude for their service. By working at the train station, Harry felt like he got to be part of that hospitality.

Miss Eileen checked her watch. "Their break time is almost up. Is the baggage car all set to go?"

Harry nodded. "Yes, ma'am." He grabbed the handle to slide the heavy door and lock it tight.

A few feet away, he saw a man in a medical corps uniform holding his wife while his daughter and son wrapped their arms around his waist. On Christmas Eve, he'd seen the same man deboard the train, drop his rucksack, and somehow manage to scoop up his daughter, hug his son, and kiss his wife in one fluid motion of joy. Now it was already time for them to say goodbye.

Harry stood beside Miss Eileen. "I wish we could give them a few more minutes." If only a family's need for a little more time could come first. But in his two years as a porter at Dennison Station, Harry had learned the importance of staying on schedule.

Miss Eileen sighed. "Here's to praying that the new year brings an end to this war."

*"I'm with you on that." It didn't seem to matter how many trains came and went, Harry still felt saddened by images of families parting ways with a father, son, or brother, and sometimes even sisters or daughters, knowing they might not return. But something about the medic with his wife and children touched him in a deep way. Maybe because he'd so recently witnessed their happy Christmas reunion.*

*He didn't recognize the family as being from Dennison, so he guessed they must be from one of the nearby towns. At least they got to be together for the holiday. The little girl, who appeared to be about six years old, had a new-looking doll in her arms. The doll's deep brown curls matched hers and her mother's.*

*"Daddy, please don't leave." The girl cried into her father's coat.*

*"I'll be back, sweetie pie." The medic cuddled the girl closer to his side and kissed the top of her head. "How about if you draw me a picture with the crayons that Santa put in your stocking?" Then he ruffled his son's hair. "We'll play ball with your new mitt when I get home."*

*"I'll practice while you're away," the boy promised.*

*Harry tried not to intrude on the private moment by staring. He distracted himself from the sad scene by* reminding other servicemen, "We're about to board." But his attention kept drifting to the man in the medical corps uniform. On Christmas Eve, Miss Eileen had mentioned that the man was a physician who'd been serving in field hospitals in Europe. Harry knew enough about the war to understand that, even for a physician assigned to the wounded, "I'll be back, sweetie pie" was a promise that fathers couldn't always keep. Lord, please keep that man safe.

Miss Eileen had her eye on the family as well. But when the conductor pointed to his pocket watch, Harry knew she couldn't put the announcement off any longer.

"All aboard," she called.

The physician gave his wife one more kiss and said goodbye to his teary daughter and his son, who was trying to be brave. Harry glanced over at the canteen table. The food was for the service members, but he would check to see if they had any extra doughnuts to cheer up the little girl and boy after the train departed. His attention shifted to the physician swinging his rucksack over his shoulder and the sound of something hitting the cold ground with a splat. A brown leather square stood out against the white of the snow.

A wallet.

*Harry ran for the wallet before it got trampled by a line of young army privates with their bagged sandwiches and steaming cups of coffee.*

*"Sir," Harry shouted. He snatched the wallet off the ground. "Excuse me." He reached the physician just as he had one foot on the train.*

*The man turned around and looked into Harry's dark brown eyes. Harry held the wallet out to him. "You dropped this, sir."*

*The man let out a big breath of relief, sending a cloud into the cold air. "Thank you, young man."*

*"I'm glad I could help, sir."*

*The man held up the wallet. "Before leaving home, I filled this thing with as many pictures of my wife and kids as I could fit inside. Right now, those are the most valuable items I own."*

*Before Harry could think of a fitting response, the medic reached into the side pocket of his rucksack and pulled out a shiny fountain pen. It was a fancy one that gentlemen carried, not an ordinary black fountain pen from the school supplies department of the drugstore. It looked like marbled copper, and the gold clip shimmered on the dreary December day. The man held it out to Harry. "Please take this as an expression of my gratitude."*

*Harry shook his head. "Oh no, sir. I couldn't take that."*

The man opened the front of Harry's coat and stuck the pen into the breast pocket of his railroad uniform. "I insist."

"But you'll need it to write home."

"I'll make do." He tipped his cap. "You're a good man. God bless you."

"God bless you too, sir." Harry tipped his hat as well.

"Happy New Year."

"Happy New Year to you too."

Then the man boarded the train. From his seat by the window, he waved to his family as the train pulled away.

Harry put his hand over the front of his coat, feeling the fountain pen through the thick wool. He looked over at Miss Eileen. He knew she'd witnessed the whole exchange when she gave him a smile of approval.

You're a good man. *No one had ever said that to him before. He felt at least five inches taller as he walked back to the depot to await the next train.*

I sure hope I can live up to that.

# CHAPTER THREE

"If only Harry were here to see this." Janet stood in front of the message board, waiting for Debbie to close the register and come over to read the note.

Debbie slipped her tip from the white-haired mystery customer into her apron pocket. "What does the note say?"

Paulette paused partway through clearing a table. "I want to see too." She hurried over.

Janet took the card down from the corkboard and faced Debbie and Paulette, unable to remove the cheesy grin from her lips. "'Harry Franklin, you truly are an inspiration to me. Write on!'"

"Aw." Debbie took the card out of Janet's hand.

Paulette read over Debbie's shoulder. "That is so sweet."

"Isn't it?" Janet tacked the card back up, right smack in the middle of the board. "Now I'm even more curious who that woman is. I've lived in Dennison my whole life and have never seen her before."

Paulette resumed busing tables. "I wish I'd been here when she came in. I could tell you if she looked familiar."

Debbie walked over to the board to post the lunch specials. "She must be new in town." She erased the breakfast items.

Janet reread the note. "I assumed that too at first. But how would she know that Harry is an inspiration based on a few minutes of watching him order a mocha and chat with us about a writing workshop?"

Debbie printed LUNCH SPECIAL in big block letters. "That is a very good point."

Janet straightened the note to Harry, debating whether to give it to him or leave it up as a public display of appreciation for one of Dennison's oldest citizens. "If she keeps coming in, January might turn out to be an eventful month after all."

"Ready for the lunch rush?" Debbie shut the door to the industrial-sized refrigerator. "At least I hope it's a rush. It'll be interesting to see how busy we are in early January. If things are steady, I thought it might be nice to ask your old friend Charla Whipple to help you with the cooking and baking once in a while."

Janet picked up a rack of freshly washed mugs to move them closer to the coffeepots. "Busy or not, I'm ready for whoever shows up. And I love the idea of having Charla around." Her former boss from the Third Street Bakery would be a fun addition to the café with her bright red lipstick and electric personality.

She had just gone through the door into the dining area and set the rack of mugs down when she spotted a petite fortysomething woman at the door.

Paulette approached her. "Feel free to sit anywhere."

"I'm looking for Janet Shaw."

Janet grabbed a clean dish towel to wipe the moisture from the mug rack off her hands. "Be right there."

Debbie came up behind her and whispered, "That's Kate Lipton. Don't let her talk you into anything." She turned to go back into the kitchen. "Be right out. I…um…noticed you're running low on white bread."

Janet took a moment to study the famous Kate Lipton while hanging the towel back on its hook. Kate looked exactly like Debbie had described her—tiny frame, light brown shoulder-length hair, and radiating with take-charge energy.

"Sorry to keep you waiting," Janet called to her.

"Janet Shaw?" Kate came over to the bakery case.

Janet pointed to herself. "That's me."

Kate extended her gloved hand. "Harry Franklin described you perfectly. I'm Kate Lipton. I'm an old friend of Debbie Albright's."

Janet shook Kate's hand. Debbie had never specifically used the words *Kate Lipton* and *friend* in the same conversation, so Janet covered her tracks with, "You must be Kate from the writing workshop Harry told us about." She could picture this woman with the commanding blue eyes motivating a roomful of senior citizens. "He was so excited about your class when he came in for coffee this morning that he took his mocha to go."

Kate took off her gloves and folded them in half. "I can already tell that Harry is going to be one of my star pupils. He was the first one to show up, with that cute dog of his, and introduced me to each person as they arrived."

"That's our Harry. It wouldn't be an exaggeration to say he knows everyone in Dennison."

Just when Janet started to wonder if Debbie planned to hide in the kitchen until Kate left, her friend came out and set a loaf of bread on the counter.

"Kate! It's so good to see you." She circled the counter to give Kate a hug. "Did you move to the area?"

"Oh goodness, no." She didn't quite wrinkle her face in disgust, but her tone communicated what she thought of the idea of leaving Cleveland for a small town with a historic train station as its only claim to fame. "My grandmother had back surgery at the beginning of December, and it wasn't as successful as we hoped. The family decided it was time for her to move to Good Shepherd Retirement Center. I could tell right away that it was going to be a rough adjustment, and my mom and her siblings are still figuring out what to do with her house, so I thought I would stick around for a few weeks to help Gran settle in. In the meantime, I'm staying at her home in Barnhill and thought I'd offer a workshop while I'm in the area."

*Thought I'd offer a workshop while I'm in the area?* Janet couldn't fathom throwing in an extra commitment while helping an elderly family member recover from a disappointing surgery and adjust to a major life change. Especially a workshop that would include students in their nineties and at least one centenarian.

Debbie's expression reminded her why she shouldn't be shocked.

Again, she played innocent. "That's a pretty ambitious undertaking."

Kate rested her purse on the counter. "I confess that my motives are mixed. The workshop will allow me to keep an eye on Gran without making it obvious that I'm doing so."

"I didn't know you were a writer," Debbie said.

Kate waved her hand. "Oh, I dabble a little. Remember, I published the women's ministries newsletter at church for quite some time."

"How could I forget *WOW News*?" Debbie turned to Janet. "*Wow* stood for Women of the Word."

Kate put her hand on Debbie's arm. "Debbie contributed recipes occasionally. Very good ones, I might add."

"That's right. I remember her mentioning those." What Janet remembered most were the frantic texts from Debbie, asking for recipe suggestions because Kate wanted something yesterday. "So, what can I do for you?" she asked their guest.

Kate peered into the bakery case. "Harry highly recommended your baked goods."

"Harry is one of our most loyal customers. In fact, I wouldn't be surprised if he wandered in with Crosby at any moment. What would you like?"

"I need refreshments for my workshop on Wednesday morning. Today I had coffee and tea available and brought some packaged cookies from the store. As my grandmother pointed out, they tasted just like the package. I was mortified. I don't bake and have no idea of the offerings around here, so I asked the group for a recommendation, and Harry raved about your café."

"Remind me what time the workshop begins?"

"Ten o'clock." Kate went back to surveying the baked treats. "I give them a short teaching segment followed by time to write their stories. This morning, my twelve students enjoyed having coffee and something to munch on while they wrote."

"Do you want me to set something aside for you to pick up before class? That won't be a problem at all."

"Actually..." Kate clasped her hands and scrunched her eyes. "I was hoping to have the order delivered to Good Shepherd. I'll be swamped with preparations before class. I would be happy to pay a delivery fee."

Janet looked to Debbie for what to do. The expression on her friend's face confirmed what Janet was already thinking. "I'm sorry, but we don't have a delivery service. We're just a small café."

"Have you considered adding delivery? It would be good for business. My workshop could be a trial."

Janet marveled over Kate's delicate blend of boldness and charm. No wonder her victims managed to dive in without knowing the depth of the water. Debbie looked dumbfounded too, and she knew Kate. They'd delivered some meals in the months since they opened the café, but always after hours. The workshop took place during one of the busiest times of the day, when many regulars popped in for coffee or a late breakfast.

The reality of turning Kate down in front of some of those customers added an extra complication to the mix.

Just when Janet was about to acquiesce, Debbie said, "That's a great idea to consider for the future, but as of today, we don't deliver. I'm sorry."

Kate slumped her shoulders and stared into the bakery case, her finger resting on her chin. She looked up with a gleam of expectancy in her eyes. "I think I have a solution. Harry mentioned that his granddaughter comes here each morning for coffee and a sweet treat. Maybe she would be willing to drop my order off? Or you can just send it with Harry? That might be even easier."

Janet cringed over Kate's suggestion that they pass the buck to either a busy professional or a ninety-five-year-old man. Would it really be that difficult for her to swing by to pick up a box of ginger-bread slices? Then she had a flashback of Harry's excitement before Kate's workshop that morning. He looked so cute with his to-go cup in one hand and Crosby's leash in the other, eager to buy his note-book and head to class so he wouldn't be tardy. He wouldn't hesitate to help out by picking up the gingerbread. *All the more reason why I don't want to ask him.*

The words flew out of Janet's mouth almost involuntarily. "I don't mind delivering the refreshments just this once."

"Really?" Kate's whole face lit up in a way that told Janet there might have been more behind the request. "Thank you so much."

Debbie shot Janet a look that said, *Aw, man. You caved.* "Are you sure, Janet?"

"Paulette will be here by then." Her stomach did a flip. *Hopefully nobody comes in actually wanting to eat at that time.* "We talked about bringing Charla on. I could ask her to cover for me." If she could come in at such short notice. "It might mean a lot to Harry and would let him know we're supporting his efforts to write his life stories. It'll give me a chance to see Eileen and Ray and check in on how they're doing. Unless you'd rather I not do it."

Kate put her arm around Debbie and gazed up at her. "Debbie. You can manage for an hour or so without Janet, right? After all, it's for a good cause."

Debbie finally found her voice. "If Charla is available to cook, I can manage. As long as Janet doesn't mind."

"For Harry's sake, I'm happy to do it. I'll drop your order off a little before ten on Wednesday."

Kate reacted with a happy little clap. "This is an answer to prayer. I had a feeling that a friend of Debbie's would be willing to serve."

Debbie's eyes said *You don't have to do this.*

Janet sent over a nonverbal *It's okay. Really.* She asked Kate, "So what would you like?"

Kate went back to examining the offerings in the bakery case. "Everything looks so good. Debbie, what do you recommend?"

"Everything that Janet bakes is spectacular. But customers especially like the gingerbread right now."

Janet opened the case. "I can give you a sample if you want to try it first. My special ingredient is a splash of pure maple syrup." She left out the little detail about adding it at the last minute one morning when she discovered she was short on molasses.

"Gingerbread sounds delicious. No need for a sample. I'll take fifteen slices." Kate pulled out her wallet. "Should I pay now or upon delivery?"

"On delivery is fine."

"You have no idea what this means to me." She put her wallet away and released a big sigh. "Now, I better get home to plan Wednesday's class."

She started fishing through her purse and wove around the tables between the counter and the exit. She stopped in front of Janet's writing station and pulled out her key fob. "This message board is a lovely idea for January when we all have the post-holiday blahs. I'll be sure to add something to the board another day when I have more than thirty seconds to spare." Then she picked up the fountain pen and gasped. She hurried back to the counter. "Debbie, I'm surprised you're keeping a fountain pen like this out in the open."

"That's Janet's. The whole idea for the writing station was hers."

Kate cradled the pen in her palm as if it were made of glass. "If you're smart, Janet," she said, "you'll put this away before it gets stolen."

Janet told herself not to be offended by Kate's sudden use of a teacher voice. "But I bought it to be used. Customers are enjoying writing with something old and different."

"This pen is a collector's item."

In her mind, Janet could see $15 handwritten on a circular blue sticker on the box the pen came in. Nothing about it left her feeling as if she'd gotten a great deal on something much more valuable. "I guess I have a few things to learn about pens. My specialty is baking. How can you tell it's valuable?"

"Because my brother-in-law is a pen collector." Kate set the pen down carefully. "He has some that are worth so much that he never uses them."

Janet replayed the previous day's visit in her mind and the moment when she spotted the glass case for expensive jewelry. *If the pen was valuable, wouldn't it have been displayed in the case too?* "I don't want to come across as rude, but I think you might be mistaken. I bought it at a consignment store over the weekend for fifteen bucks."

"Then the person who sold it to you didn't know pens either." Kate waved Debbie over to the counter. She turned her back to the customers and spoke in a hushed tone that one might use when sharing her bank account or Social Security number. "See this dark copper color? It's called copper pearl." She pointed to the barrel of the pen. "It isn't even listed in the Parker catalog. Parker released so few of these that only a handful exist." She tapped the top of the pen. "Parker invented the button ink filler under this cap. It's one thing that gives your pen away as a vintage Parker Duofold. But the color is what makes it so valuable."

Janet picked up the pen for a closer look. "You really know your writing instruments."

"To be fair, my brother-in-law was admiring a pen like this one during the holidays, so it's fresh in my mind. When I visited for Christmas, he took us into one of those stationery stores where people are willing to pay as much for pens as they do for major appliances, and the seller had a copper-pearl Parker Duofold behind glass. Like this one, it had signs of wear. It was priced at eighteen hundred dollars." She nodded to the pen in Janet's hand. "Lance would snatch that up in a heartbeat. If you insist on letting customers write with it, I recommend at least keeping it behind the counter and letting only people you trust use it."

Janet thought about Harry's reaction to seeing the pen and the mystery white-haired customer who wrote so beautifully with it. She wasn't convinced that the pen was worth much more than the fifteen dollars she'd paid for it. "It seems unnecessary to keep it hidden away and make our customers ask permission to use it." Of course, it would also be a shame to have it stolen.

Kate slipped on her gloves. "At least put it away after you close each day."

"That's my plan." Janet followed Kate to the exit and returned the pen to its box. "We'll be careful. I promise."

While preparing to close the café, Janet pulled a tray of muffins out of the bakery case so she could transfer them into a container to sell as day-olds the next morning. "Eighteen hundred dollars for a pen? That's insane."

Debbie looked up from the counter where she was recording the day's receipts. "You'd be surprised how much people are willing to pay for something with *RARE* written in all caps in the description." She leaned back in her chair. "Based on what I remember about Kate, I wouldn't be shocked if she's embellishing a bit. I don't mean to be critical, but she has a tendency to talk big when it comes to brands and the quality of pricey items. I doubt the owner of Aunt Maggie's would have sold the pen for such a low price if it was a collector's item."

Janet snapped the container shut. "Anne did say that pens aren't her area of expertise. I obviously don't know the difference between a high-end fountain pen and a cheap one either. My grandparents always owned at least one fountain pen, but they stuck with the Parker 51, especially after hearing that Eisenhower used one to sign the German Instrument of Surrender." Janet looked over her shoulder at the shiny marbled fountain pen. It had only been out for a day, but more customers had chosen to use it over the colored gel pens and the ballpoints. No one else had pointed it out as something valuable. They just thought it was fun to use. Kate's reaction to seeing it out in the open replayed in Janet's mind. "Kate was so concerned about us keeping it out. You'd think it was hers."

Debbie rested her arms on the table. "That seemed a little over-the-top to me too. Even for Kate."

"Harry said he used to have one like it." Janet drummed her fingers on the container of leftover muffins. "I guess it wouldn't hurt to research its value."

"We can always ask Kim tomorrow." Debbie shut her laptop. "Now I'm fascinated. Who knew a pen could be such a big deal?"

# CHAPTER FOUR

The next morning, Kim Smith, the curator of the depot museum, came into the café with a friendly "Good morning." She sat on the stool beside Patricia and eyed her peppermint mocha and square of coffee cake.

Patricia held up her cup. "Do you want the same? You won't be sorry."

Kim smacked her hips. "I might be when I see the numbers on the scale. I better stick with regular coffee and skim milk today. It's time for my jeans to recover from the holidays."

Janet gave Kim an empathetic pout. "Isn't the post-holiday calorie-conscious reality a drag?"

"It's the worst part of January." Kim folded her hands on the counter and leaned forward. "You know what is fun though? Seeing my hundred-year-old mom embrace the New Year by taking a writing workshop."

Janet hit the button on the coffee maker to start a fresh pot. "Harry is taking that class too. He looked like a kid on his first day of school yesterday."

Patricia wrapped both hands around her mug. "He called me last night to read a story to me. I can't remember the last time I heard him sound so excited over something besides trains and the history of Dennison."

"I went to visit Mom yesterday, and she couldn't stop talking about Kate Lipton. She couldn't wait to get started on her first story." A look of sadness clouded Kim's eyes. "Her arthritis is bad right now because of the cold weather, so I had her dictate her story to me to type up on my laptop. I printed it and drove it over to her." She reached for a packet of sugar substitute. "Between Mom, Harry, Ray, and others in the community, I imagine Kate will end up with some great stories."

"That settles it. I want to support their efforts too." Janet put her hand on her hip. "Not only will I deliver the refreshments for every class session, but I'm going to talk to Debbie about us donating them. It can be our community service to the class."

Debbie came over with a breakfast order from a foursome of community-college students who were engaged in a lively debate at a table in the back. "I'm way ahead of you, girlfriend. I was thinking the same thing. Maybe Harry can take requests for next week's refreshments."

"Yes. He'll love the idea of having a job." Janet set Kim's coffee in front of her along with a small pitcher of milk. With all the customers served and nobody waiting at the door, this seemed like a perfect time to ask her about the fountain pen. "Do you mind taking a look at something while you're drinking your coffee?"

Kim stirred the sweetener into her coffee. "Not at all."

Janet noticed the interest in Patricia's eyes as she sat quietly sipping her mocha. "You might enjoy this too, Patricia."

She went to the writing desk to retrieve the pen and brought it over to Kim. "I bought this at a consignment store the other day. Yesterday a woman came in and informed me that it's a collector's item."

Kim picked up the pen and examined it closely. "You found this at a consignment shop?"

"Yep." She told Kim what she paid for it.

"This is worth a lot more than fifteen dollars." Kim unscrewed the cap.

Patricia scooted in closer. "I didn't get a good look at the pen yesterday, but now that it's right in front of me, I can tell it's high quality." She touched the *Made in USA* stamp on the barrel. "Part of the *M* is rubbed off, but that's just normal wear and tear."

Debbie finished pouring coffee for the college debaters and came over to join the discussion.

Kim inspected the nib. "I can tell from the weight and design that this isn't your run-of-the-mill fountain pen. And the nib is stamped fourteen-karat gold. That's not a detail that the average person would look for, so it's not surprising that you didn't notice. Do you want me to help you research the value?"

"I would appreciate that a lot."

Kim whipped out her phone and took a picture of the pen. "I'll look it up today and get back to you. I'm not expecting any field trips or groups at the museum, so I'll have time."

"I'll be anxious to hear what you find out."

Janet took the pen from Kim and felt the weight of it in her hand. She examined the gold nib. *Maybe I should put it away after all.* Then she glanced up and saw Harry coming toward the entrance with Crosby at his heels. He looked forward to using it for his stories. For his sake, she decided to keep it out.

She returned it to its place of honor beside the lap desk. As soon as Harry walked in, Janet's mind shifted from the fountain pen to a certain note he hadn't yet seen. She waited until he unzipped his coat before announcing, "Harry Franklin, you have a secret admirer, and it isn't even Valentine's Day."

He stopped in his tracks. "I do? I haven't had an admirer since Sylvia passed."

"Well, you have one now." Janet nodded toward the message board. "Take a gander at that cream-colored card in the middle."

Harry looked down at Crosby. "Come on, ol' boy. Let's see who's flirting with me."

Janet sat down beside Patricia and watched.

Harry leaned over the desk to read his note. His shoulders straightened. "I'm an inspiration?" He tapped his finger on the note. "Patricia, did you write this?"

Patricia started gathering her things. "Wasn't me."

Janet picked up Patricia's credit card. "It wasn't any of us. Remember that stylish white-haired lady who was making eyes at you before you left for class yesterday morning? It was her."

"I don't recall anyone making eyes at me. But I do remember noticing the lady with white hair." He took down the note and showed it to Crosby. "Look at that. We're an inspiration." He tacked it back up. "I didn't do anything inspiring while she was here."

On her way to the kitchen, Debbie called, "You inspired her simply by being you."

Janet took Patricia's credit card to the register. "I think she's sweet on you, Harry."

He led Crosby to a table near Patricia and Kim. "I don't know about her being sweet on me. If she was, wouldn't she have come over to say hello instead of leaving a note on the wall for everybody to see?"

Janet thought about that. He did have a point. Still, it was fun to consider the prospect of someone having her eye on Harry Franklin. His wife, Sylvia, had been gone for over ten years. "Maybe she's shy."

Harry folded his arms. "She didn't seem shy to me."

Janet recalled the woman's confident posture and voice and the way she surveyed the café as if taking in every detail of it. "You're right about that. But maybe she's shy about speaking to men she doesn't know."

Patricia went up behind Harry and put her hands on his shoulders and her cheek close to his. "Or maybe she's waiting for the right moment to return to the café and ask you out on a date."

Harry patted his granddaughter's cheek then unhooked Crosby's leash. "Oh, now you girls are just being goofy. Whether she's sweet on me or not, that's a really encouraging note she left."

Debbie came into the dining area, balancing four plates in her arms. She dropped them off at the college students' table. "I heard you ladies out here giving Harry a hard time. Can I join in?"

Patricia gave Harry a half hug. "I better get to work, Pop Pop. Keep me updated on your winter romance."

Harry gave Debbie a pleading expression that made Janet want to crack up. "Come rescue me, Debbie."

Debbie pulled an order pad out of her pocket. "I'm here for you, buddy. What can I do to help?"

He picked up a menu. "I thought I'd treat myself to something different for breakfast today. I was up late last night writing my memoirs. What sort of sustenance would you recommend after such an activity?"

Debbie smiled. "How about the special?"

"Does the special have any trendy superfoods in it?"

"Not a bit. It's cinnamon French toast with cream cheese drizzle and a choice of bacon, sausage, or ham."

"Sounds delicious." He handed over his menu. "I'll take the special with bacon."

"Good choice," Debbie said. "Careful, girls, or you'll end up in his book."

"Yeah." Harry's eyes gleamed with mischief.

Kim reacted with a hearty laugh. "Okay, we'll lay off. I need to do a few things before I open the museum anyway." She set some cash on the table and held up her phone. "I'll get back to you with that information later today."

Janet took Kim's cash to the register. "So, Harry, how was your writing class? Kim said Eileen had a great time."

"Talking about writing is more like it." He leaned back in his chair and stroked Crosby's head. "That Kate Lipton is a good teacher. For the first day, she had us write about a happy childhood memory. So last night I wrote about the day my dad surprised me with a kitten. I fell down running home from school on the last day of second grade and broke my wrist. Dad showed up after work with a black-and-white female from a litter that someone was giving away outside the market. I can still recall her sweet meow and gentle purr and how she cheered me up during that summer when I couldn't swim because of my cast. I named her Cookie because she was black-and-white like one of those packaged sandwich cookies. That seems like a funny name now. But seeing as I was only about seven at the time, I suppose I could've chosen something worse. Cookie was my first pet."

Janet felt her eyes mist over as she listened to Harry tell his story. "How kind of your dad to give you a pet to cheer you up."

"It certainly was, especially when you consider that we didn't have any extra money to speak of. Cookie was a good mouser. My mother appreciated that. It's nice to remember these good things from the past. At my age, I'm well aware that not everyone has as many happy memories to look back on as I do."

Harry's face glowed in a way that Janet had never seen before. Suddenly, she could see him as a little boy, snuggled in bed with his new furry friend, his wrist in a cast. It was a nice reminder that elderly friends like Harry and Eileen and Ray were once innocent children, restless teenagers, and young adults trying to stay hopeful during tumultuous times.

"Next, I think I'll write about the day I got my fountain pen," he said. "Seeing that one over there brought it all back. That seems writerly, don't you think?"

"Very writerly." Janet set a mug of coffee in front of Harry. "You won't believe what I found out about that pen." She sat beside Harry while Debbie went to the kitchen to make his French toast. "It might be a collector's item. At least according to Kate Lipton. She came in yesterday to request baked goods for the writing workshop and discouraged me from keeping it out in the open."

Harry turned toward the writing desk. "It's pretty amazing when you think about it. Whenever we buy something secondhand, we're buying an item with a story behind it."

"If you still have your pen somewhere, it might be worth something too. I'll let you know what I find out."

Harry reached for his coffee. "Nah, I gave mine away a long time ago, to someone who needed it more than I did."

Janet was thankful for the lull so she could sit with Harry for a few minutes. Between the fountain pen and the note, she sensed that she had a lot to learn about the big-hearted retired conductor who enjoyed watching the trains go by. "Now that I know you might have owned something fancy, I'm even more curious. Did you get the fountain pen as an award?" If Harry truly owned a rare Parker Duofold, even at one time, Janet couldn't picture him buying it for himself. He wasn't a high-end sort of man.

Debbie came out with Harry's breakfast and set it in front of him. Janet pulled out the chair beside her own, encouraging her friend to take advantage of the chance to take a break and hear Harry's story.

Harry shook open a napkin and laid it in his lap. "I guess you could call it an award. I got it from a physician who served in the medical corps during the war." Harry's eyes drifted toward the writing station. "It was 1944, right after Christmas. I can still see him with his wife and children, promising them he would be back. He dropped his wallet while rushing to board the train. I picked it up and returned it to him, and he gave me his fountain pen as a thank-you. 'You're a good man,' he said. He slipped it right into my breast pocket." Harry put his hand over his chest for a moment as if he could still feel the pen in his pocket. "After the train pulled out, I watched his wife put one arm around her daughter and her other arm around her son and suggest that they go home and write a letter to Daddy. I didn't know his name, but after that, I prayed each day that he would be able to keep his promise to come back." He picked up his knife and fork. "I didn't see him or his family again. I don't know what became of him, but I think he would approve of my choice to pass that nice pen on to someone else."

"You should definitely write that story, Harry." Janet got up from the table. "It's wonderful."

"Yeah, it's one of those moments that's etched in my memory even though I don't have the pen anymore. It meant a lot to me that he saw me as a good man."

Janet reached out and patted his arm. "I'm glad that physician saw the real you."

Harry cut into his French toast.

Janet glanced at the pen. If Harry gave his away… "Who did you give your pen to?"

"A girl." He took a bite of his breakfast and chewed with his eyes closed. "*Mm-mm.* This hits the spot." He picked up a piece of bacon. "I better let you ladies get back to work."

The sound of the door opening alerted Janet to the arrival of a new wave of customers, but she could have sat at Harry's table listening to him all morning. Giving a prized possession away to someone who needed it more than he did was so like him. "Well, you can use our fountain pen as often as you like."

Debbie went over to welcome an incoming couple and show them to a table.

Harry held Crosby back from running to greet them. "I'd like that. Maybe I'll sign each story that I write with the pen. You know, for a personal touch, like an autograph."

"There you go." Janet straightened her apron. "Or you can write your first drafts with it here at the café."

Harry wiped his mouth and pushed away from the table. "For now, I think I'll use it to write a message for your board."

He got up and strolled to the writing desk with Crosby close behind. He picked up the fountain pen and studied it for a moment before rummaging through the desk for a note card. He sat in the chair, looked up at the ceiling, let out an "*Ah*," and then started writing. After a minute or two, Harry returned the pen to its box, selected a tack, and pinned his card to the board.

"There you are. My words of wisdom for the day." He shuffled back to his table.

Janet walked over to read what Harry had written.

"*Stories are powerful things. And yours just might make a difference.*" ~ Kate Lipton

She noticed the pride on his face over sharing something other than *Choose joy* or *Have a nice day*. "I totally agree, Harry."

"That's something Kate told us yesterday. It really motivated me. I never thought of personal stories as something powerful. Apparently, mine might be."

"I have a feeling they will be too."

Janet and Debbie were cleaning up after a slow lunchtime, which had prompted them to send Paulette home early, when Kim came back into the café. Janet set aside her spray cleaner and roll of paper towels. "Hi, Kim. Are you here for lunch?"

"No, I need to show you something."

As Kim pulled out her phone, the café door opened again, and in walked Harry's admirer.

"Ah, man," Janet said under her breath. "Too bad Harry isn't here." She held up one finger. "Hold that thought, Kim. I'll be right with you."

She picked up a menu. "Welcome back."

"Nice to be back." The woman loosened her green plaid scarf and nodded to the table she'd used on Monday. "I think I'll sit by the window again. I enjoy the view of the old station."

"Of course." Janet led the way to a two-person table and brought over some water. "When you were here yesterday, I didn't get a chance to introduce myself. I'm Janet Shaw."

The woman held out her hand. "Roberta Daley."

"Nice to meet you."

Roberta took off her coat and scarf and looked around the dining room. "It's nice to see this depot being put to good use again."

"Do you live around here? I don't remember seeing you before this week."

"Yes and no. I spent my childhood in Dennison then moved around a bit. Now I live in San Francisco. I came to Barnhill to spend New Year's with a friend and decided to stay for a few weeks to help her with a project."

Janet looked at Kim waiting at the counter and suddenly felt torn between Kim's news and finding a good segue into asking Roberta about her note to Harry. "It's always fun to connect with friends, isn't it?"

"It is indeed. Now I get to come here and make new ones." She took a quick peek at the menu. "What's your soup of the day?"

"Homemade minestrone."

"I'll have the soup-and-half-sandwich combo with ham on wheat, please."

"I'll get that started for you right away." Janet went to the kitchen, prepared Roberta's sandwich, and stirred the pot of minestrone to distribute the goodness that had settled to the bottom. She ladled a generous portion into a soup cup, added a packet of crackers and a pickle to the plate, and took Roberta's lunch to the table. "If you need anything else, just let me know."

Roberta examined the contents of her plate and bowl as if appreciating a gourmet meal. "This looks delicious. Thank you."

"Bon appétit."

Janet returned to her spot behind the counter and parked herself right next to Kim. "So, what did you find out?"

Kim held up her phone. "I did some research on your fountain pen, and Kate was right. When I entered the model number—it's called a Parker Duofold Senior, by the way—your copper-pearl model came up on a collector's website as a rare find." She enlarged the image on her screen. "This online seller is asking almost two thousand dollars for one, and the description says it has some signs of wear. That means it would be worth more in mint condition. Yours has signs of wear as well, but I'd say it's similar to the one pictured here."

Janet picked up Kim's phone for a closer look. "So Kate wasn't exaggerating."

"Most likely not."

Janet couldn't take her eyes off the photo on the screen. Other than some wear around the *Parker Duofold* stamp on the barrel, the pen was an exact match to the one she'd bought from Aunt Maggie's Antiques and Consignment. "How is that possible? I mean, it's a nice pen, but almost two thousand dollars?"

Kim tapped her screen again and pulled up another image. "I looked into the seller, and he's legit. He also has a Parker Duofold Big Red pen that Parker released for the fiftieth anniversary of the end of World War II to match the one that General MacArthur used to sign the surrender agreement with Japan. It already sold, but he was selling that pen for sixteen hundred. So your model is worth even more than the commemorative Douglas MacArthur fountain pen."

Janet let out a breathy, "Whoa. And to think I just got it because it was pretty and reminded me of my grandma."

"I know the price sounds unreal. But fountain pens were a big deal back when a person couldn't buy a twenty-four pack of ballpoints in the same shopping trip as an industrial-sized bag of coffee beans and a month's supply of paper products. Usually, a fountain pen was a person's only pen. The high-end ones were a sign of wealth. Fathers even passed them down to their children." Kim rested her elbows on the counter and looked at the writing table. "Some are worth far more than yours. Kate has a point that we should be careful with that one."

Janet thought about how nonchalantly Anne included it with the lap desk. Surely it was only fair to let her know. "I'll be very careful. Harry is looking forward to using it for his stories, so I don't want anything to happen to it."

Just as Kim got up, Debbie came to the counter and picked up the carafe of hot water. "I'll see if Roberta wants a warm-up on her tea," she said.

Janet took the carafe from her. "I'll do it. Kim, tell Debbie what you told me."

When she approached the table, Roberta was jotting something down in a small leather notebook.

"Can I warm up your tea?"

"That would be wonderful. Thank you." She put her notebook in her purse.

"Can I get you a fresh tea bag?"

"No, this is perfect."

"If you change your mind, I'm right over there." She returned to the counter.

"Hey, Janet," Debbie said, "what if the fountain pen you bought used to be Harry's?"

Kim took a sip of her coffee. "It's funny you should say that, because I've been wondering the same thing since hearing he had one like it. The website I just showed you said only a handful were made."

Janet tried to remember Harry's stories from that morning. "He said he gave it away. But if he gave it to someone who stayed in the area, it could've easily found its way to a consignment shop."

Kim put her phone in her pocket. "Right. Because if Parker only released a few of these pens, what are the chances of two of them ending up in or around Dennison, Ohio?"

At that moment, Janet wanted to box up the pen and hide it in the back room to only take out for Harry to use. But she knew that wasn't what he would want.

When she'd made the decision to let customers use the pen for the message board, she'd done it with the plan that she would take it home at the end of January. But now that it might be Harry's, a new idea came to mind. "Even if it isn't Harry's, I think I want to give him the pen after we put the message board away."

Kim checked her watch. "I love that idea. It would mean so much to him. Especially after taking on the challenge of writing."

Roberta called Janet's name from her table. "Pardon me for interrupting, but the friend I'm staying with just called in a bit of a crisis and needs some help. May I take the rest of my lunch to go? And if I can have a second cup of soup for my friend, I would appreciate it."

Janet moved off the stool. "Of course."

Kim headed toward the door. "I need to go anyway. We can talk more later."

Janet masked her disappointment over seeing Roberta leave so quickly. She reached under the counter for some to-go containers. *Will I ever find out this woman's connection to Harry?*

# CHAPTER FIVE

*April 7, 1945*

"Hey, Harry, your girlfriend's here."

Harry ignored his fellow porter, Mitch's, comment. He'd gotten used to the lanky ten-year-old girl with the golden-brown hair following him around Dennison Station on Saturdays. Her name was Birdie, and she'd been coming to the station since the weather warmed up and her older sister started volunteering at the Salvation Army canteen. Birdie always wore the same messenger hat, a too-large boy's blazer over her dress, regardless of the temperature, and a Kodak camera around her neck.

According to Miss Eileen, the girls' father had been injured in France and their oldest sister served as a nurse in the Pacific. Harry's guess was, Birdie tagged *along with her sister to give their mother a chance to care for their father while he recovered without being shadowed by a child whose favorite hobby seemed to be peppering people with questions. And Birdie had a lot of questions. She recorded the answers in the composition book she carried under her arm. So far, she had "interviewed" Harry about when he started working at Dennison Station, what he liked most about being a porter, his favorite movies, and how he got the fountain pen that she saw him using one day. Today she had a new composition book, so he prepared himself for another question-and-answer session.*

*"Afternoon, Harry." Birdie pulled a stubby pencil out of her blazer pocket.*

*"Afternoon, Birdie."*

*Harry stood at the edge of the platform and watched for the train that was due to arrive any minute. If Birdie stuck to her typical routine, as soon as servicemen and women deboarded, she would turn her attention from Harry to those standing in line for food at the canteen.*

*Birdie walked up beside Harry. "Can I try out your fountain pen? I want to write my name inside my new notebook."*

*Part of him wanted to tell Birdie to use her pencil instead. What if she pressed too hard on the nib or* dropped the pen and it rolled off the platform onto the train tracks? But when Birdie looked up at him with pleading eyes, he couldn't bring himself to be greedy. Birdie made it clear almost every time she came to Dennison Station that she was the official reporter in residence. If she ever became a famous writer, Harry didn't want to show up in one of her stories as the mean porter who wouldn't let her try out his fountain pen. He opened the front of his jacket and pulled out the pearly copper pen. "Sure. As long as you stay right here and promise to be careful with it."

"I promise." Birdie held out her hand, and Harry passed the pen to her.

Her lips parted when she took it from him, and her eyes got a twinkle in them. "This is the nicest pen I've ever seen. When I become a writer, I will never use a pencil again, only a fountain pen." She went to sit on the bench behind her and twisted off the cap. "Or a typewriter, of course."

"Tell you what, Birdie. When you publish your first book, you let me know, and I'll get you a nice fountain pen to celebrate."

Birdie's eye shone. "That's a deal!"

She crossed her ankles and flipped her black-and-white composition book open. Across the top of the inside cover, she wrote Birdie L. Cummings.

Harry read over her shoulder. "That looks very professional."

"That's exactly how I'm going to autograph my books when I get famous." She screwed the lid back onto Harry's pen and looked at it with awe one more time. She moved her composition book to the bench, set Harry's pen on top of it, poised her camera, and took a picture.

"Birdie. Why are you taking a picture of my pen?"

"Because I like pens." She handed it to him. "Thanks a lot, Harry."

Harry forced himself not to tease her about taking a picture of a pen. "You're welcome." While he was returning the pen to his pocket, he saw a skinny form in the distance near the maintenance yard. Harry strained to see who it was. The man in old clothes ducked behind a freight car waiting to be repaired.

Birdie turned the page in her composition book. "Harry, do you have a sweetheart?" She held her pencil over the page.

The man peeked out from behind the freight car. He wore a red woolen cap and looked like he needed a shave and a haircut.

"Harry?"

Birdie forced his gaze away from the raggedy man. Most men were either in Europe or the Pacific.

*This man didn't look old enough to stay behind because of his age. Whatever his reason for hanging around the station instead of fighting in the war, his clothes gave away that he was down on his luck, and men in that kind of situation wouldn't want people staring. He memorized the man's appearance. Miss Eileen would want to know about someone hanging around the freight cars.*

*"Harry?"*

*He'd forgotten her question. "What's that, Birdie?"*

*"Do you have a sweetheart?"*

*Harry turned his attention back to watching for the incoming train. "Not at the moment." Not ever, if he had to be honest.*

*"You should have a sweetheart," Birdie said. "You're a nice person."*

*"That's nice of you, Birdie. Thanks." He listened for the train whistle, wishing he'd seen where the man in the cap had run off to.*

*"Birdie!" Birdie's sister shouted at her from the coffee-service table at the end of the platform. "Stop pestering Harry while he's working."*

*Without turning around, Birdie hollered back, "I'm not pestering him." She wrote something in her book. Harry assumed it was something along the lines of* Harry Franklin is in need of a sweetheart.

Harry took a few steps toward the canteen. "It's okay," he called. "She isn't bothering me."

The distant whistle of the train cued Harry to stop concerning himself with anything but the passengers and their luggage. "I need to get back to work now."

Birdie hopped down from the bench. "Me too. I have servicemen to interview as soon as the train gets here. They have intriguing stories. You should talk to them sometime."

She took off before Harry could explain that talking to the servicemen, aside from answering questions and wishing them well, would keep him from doing his job.

Miss Eileen approached Harry as a blast of engine smoke announced the train's arrival. Telling her about the man in the red stocking cap would have to wait. Harry made his way to the baggage car and spotted the red-cap man casually walking toward the depot and into the crowd of passengers.

# CHAPTER SIX

**W**hen Janet got out of her car at Good Shepherd Retirement Center on Wednesday morning, she took a moment to enjoy the peaceful beauty of the property. The paved paths and outdoor benches were empty due to the cold, but the maintenance crew had still taken time to clear away snow and any moisture that could cause a person of any age to slip. The giant snowcapped pine trees added to the welcoming feel of the residence where she so often visited her friends Eileen and Ray.

She smoothed the plastic wrap over her plate of icing-drizzled gingerbread and walked the familiar halls to the activities room. If she hurried, she could get back to the café in time to keep her promise of "I'll only be thirty minutes, tops." Charla had already made herself at home in the café kitchen, but she didn't want to leave her on her own for too long.

"Hello there, stranger." Harry's voice broke her out of her on-a-mission pace. He stood right outside the activities room with Ray Zink. Crosby had poised himself beside Ray's wheelchair for some affection. Harry had a red spiral notebook under his arm, completing his resemblance to a star pupil who couldn't wait to nab his spot in the front row of class.

"Hi, Harry. Hello there, Ray."

Ray looked up, his hand still on Crosby's back. "What are you doing here? Are you joining us for class?"

She raised her plate. "I'm dropping off snacks."

Harry took hold of the door handle for the activities room. "Everyone who didn't sign up for the class is going to be so jealous now." He swept his arm in an after-you fashion as if reliving his days working for the railroad.

Janet caught the strap of her tote bag before it slipped down her arm. "Always the gentleman. Thank you, Harry."

She found Kate flying from one round table to the next, distributing stacks of papers and cups filled with pens. One elderly woman stood near the front of the room, supported by a walker and engulfed in an overly large blue cardigan, watching Kate's every move.

Along the wall, Janet found a long table that had already been stocked with two small carafes, pitchers of water, paper cups, and a basket of creamers, sweeteners, and stir sticks. "Good morning. I come bearing goodies." She set her plate down and started peeling back the plastic wrap.

Kate dropped her stack of papers and hurried over with her arms open. "Good morning, my friend."

Janet let go of the plastic wrap to accept Kate's embrace. *We're friends already? I had no idea.* "I'm always happy to provide baked goods."

Kate gripped Janet's arms and looked straight into her eyes. "You're an angel."

An attendant pushed Ray's wheelchair into the room. Eileen and Harry walked in behind them. Janet waved to the group.

She reached into her tote bag to retrieve a stack of leftover red napkins from Christmas. "I brought these, just in case."

Kate put her hands over the pockets of her gray pants and her sweater then reached under the table and pulled out her purse. "How much do I owe you?"

"Nothing at all." It felt surprisingly good to say that after the pressure of Kate's request two days ago. "Debbie and I talked about it, and we want to donate the refreshments." She waited for Kate to protest.

Instead, Kate put her fingertips over her lips and sucked in her breath. Her eyes had a hint of sadness mixed with genuine gratitude. "Thank you."

"Consider it our way of supporting everyone's writing efforts." Janet set the napkins down and fanned them out. "I better say a quick hello to my friends and get back to the café. Feel free to return the plate whenever it's convenient."

"Of course. Thanks again."

When Janet went over to say hello to Eileen, her friend appeared to be going out of her way to engage the woman with the walker in a conversation.

"Janet," Eileen said as soon as she locked eyes with her, "this is Nora, Kate's grandmother. She just moved in with us."

Janet started to extend her hand then noticed how tightly Nora gripped her walker. She saw the woman giving her I BAKE BECAUSE IT'S CHEAPER THAN THERAPY sweatshirt a critical eye. "Welcome to the Good Shepherd family, Nora."

Kate's grandmother turned up one corner of her mouth. "I've never seen anything quite like this place before."

Janet nodded, trying to figure out if Nora's comment was meant as a compliment or a slam. "You've found a good friend in Eileen."

Crosby came over and stood at Nora's feet. She looked down at him. "Yes, I see you there, trying to steal the show like you did on Monday."

Harry smacked his leg. "Come on, Crosby. Leave Nora alone." He led his dog to a table front and center near Kate's teaching podium and giant whiteboard.

An attendant came in and pulled Kate aside.

Janet looked at the clock on the wall. Almost ten. She needed to go. She said goodbye to Eileen and was on her way over to Harry and Ray when she felt a gentle tap on her arm. She turned around and saw Kate standing with her hands clasped in front of her.

"Could I borrow you for a moment?"

Janet glanced at the clock again. "Sure. I can talk for a quick sec."

She followed Kate to the front corner of the room and prepared herself for another food-related request. She had an answer planned in advance: *I need to ask Debbie and get back to you.* Janet overheard Eileen inviting Nora to sit with her. Other class participants from Good Shepherd and the community trickled in. She took comfort in knowing the workshop was about to start and Kate wouldn't have time to talk her into anything unreasonable. But as soon as she looked at Kate's face and saw that distress had overtaken the joy of free refreshments, she started bracing herself.

Kate put her hand on Janet's arm and leaned in so close that Janet could tell she was chewing spearmint gum. "Is there any way you can stick around for a few minutes? I desperately need some help."

Janet guessed she wanted help passing out the gingerbread and prayed she was correct. "Okay." She turned toward the refreshments table.

Kate caught her elbow. "Some of the older ones are having trouble getting their stories from their heads to the paper and feel overwhelmed. I underestimated how difficult that would be, managing on my own. Yesterday, I got a call from Good Shepherd asking me to come up with a plan to make the class more, um, elderly friendly. A friend encouraged me to get some volunteers to help those who need someone to transcribe their stories. She's coming today, and Good Shepherd offered an assistant as well. But I was just informed that the assistant they chose is home with a sick child. If you could stay and provide reinforcements, I'd be forever grateful."

Panic shot through Janet's body. Based on the rising volume in the room, Kate's students were getting restless. But Janet had told Debbie and Charla she would be gone for half an hour, not half the morning. Did Kate really think she could leave them to run things by themselves without notice? The café hadn't been very busy when she left, but that could have changed. What if a big group came in, or something happened that required as many hands as possible? "I'm sorry, but Debbie and the woman covering the kitchen are expecting me."

"Debbie will understand. Trust me. She's a gem."

"I know she is. But—"

Kate took Janet's hand. "The thing is, if residents continue to feel like this is too much for them, Good Shepherd will consider pulling the workshop from the schedule." Her voice started to quiver. "I had something exciting planned for today, and canceling will be a big disappointment for those who are truly enjoying it. People like Eileen and your friend Harry."

From Debbie's stories, Janet knew Kate could be persistent and even a tad manipulative. But today she seemed to truly be in a bind. Janet looked around at the eager group of elderly memoirists, sitting at their tables with pens and paper, electronic tablets, or laptops. Kate had said she had twelve students, and there were twelve people in the room, so despite any frustrations with getting words to paper, all her students had showed up today. And considering the familiar faces in the room who were either heading toward or had already reached the century mark, Kate definitely had her hands full.

Eileen smiled at Janet from across the room. "Janet, are you staying today?"

*How can I say no to that?* She reached into her tote bag. "I need a minute to contact Debbie and make sure Charla can stick around."

"Oh yes, please feel free. I'm doing a short teaching segment first anyway." Kate shoved an electronic tablet into Janet's hands and pointed her to Nora. "When writing time begins, I'll assign you to Gran and Eileen." Kate smoothed her hair and closed her eyes for a moment. Relief showed on her face. "Thank you."

"No problem." *Okay, that's not exactly true.*

She found Debbie's number while making her way around Harry's table and dropped her tote bag beside the chair between Eileen and Nora.

Nora took a blank legal pad out of the front pocket of her walker and smacked it down on the table. "So I'm being shoved off on you now, am I?"

Janet brushed off the comment and looked up from her phone. "Consider me your personal scribe for the morning."

Nora fished through the pocket of her oversized cardigan and pulled out a white pen with the Good Shepherd Retirement Center logo on it. "*Oh-kay.*"

Eileen leaned forward and whispered to Janet, "Nora likes to act spicy, but she is actually a very nice person."

Janet put her hand on Nora's arm. It felt so frail. "I look forward to getting to know you, Nora."

"*Humph.* We'll see if you feel the same at the end of class."

Janet noted the hint of mischief in her eyes.

"Can I bring you some gingerbread?"

Nora settled herself back in the folding chair. "No thanks. I don't care for gingerbread."

While Kate called the group to order and announced the topic for the day—*Life's Defining Moments*—Janet took advantage of the opportunity to text Debbie.

She sensed Nora watching her as her thumbs flew.

So sorry. Looks like I'll be a while. Can you ask Charla if she can stay?

Nora muttered, "Teacher, Janet is texting in class."

Janet laughed. "She knows I'm just telling Debbie where I am."

A *ding* alerted her to Debbie's quick reply.

Not a problem. Everything okay over there?

Kate needs my help. I'll explain later.

She hit send, sat up straight, and made eye contact with Kate.

Kate set her dry-erase marker in the tray of the whiteboard and clapped her hands together. "Now I have a surprise for all of you."

Eileen looked across the table at Janet, her eyes wide with delight.

Nora lowered her head. Under her breath she said, "But wait, there's more."

Kate didn't skip a beat. "We are going to write a book together."

The joy that took over the room lightened Janet's fear that she was abandoning her best friend.

Then Nora burst the bubble. "By the end of January, Kate? Please explain how you'll pull that off."

Janet wanted to ask the same thing, but maybe in a more discreet way. She knew, based on her mother's long career as an editor, that it took longer than four weeks to publish a book.

"I'm glad you asked, Gran." Kate wrote *Wednesday, January 24*, on the whiteboard. "That's the beauty of local print shops. I already called around and found one with a twenty-four-hour turnaround. Each of you is invited to contribute a story, or more if you really get inspired, and get it to me by two weeks from today."

A woman Janet recognized as a Good Shepherd resident raised her hand. "Can I write poems? My stories keep coming out as poems."

"Of course. You can write in any form you want—as a poem, as a play, even as a series of pictures with creative captions. Tell your story any way it comes out. Have fun with this. In the meantime, I'll design a cover." She gestured to Janet. "And Janet and I will be here to help you."

Janet looked around and smiled awkwardly. "Just for today."

Nora pointed at her. "Ha ha. My granddaughter's got you in her grip now."

Kate picked up a paper. "This sheet is filled with ideas and tips for getting your story finished in time. My other assistant is coming to help anyone who needs it. She should be here any minute."

The door opened in such a perfectly timed fashion that it almost felt staged.

"And there she is. My friend Roberta is here to help as well."

Harry shifted around in his chair. Janet expected him to say a friendly, "Hello again," as soon as he recognized the familiar face from the café. Instead, his welcoming posture stiffened for a moment. He offered a tentative wave as Roberta Daley greeted the class, took off her coat, and found a place to sit.

Janet's shoulders slumped at the sight of Harry's sudden self-consciousness. Maybe she shouldn't have teased him about having a secret admirer. It seemed now he felt uneasy around her.

She shifted in her seat, wishing she'd had the courage to turn down Kate's request so she could drive back to her happy place in the café's kitchen.

Janet hurried into the café and grabbed her current favorite apron with the polka dots. She swept her hand across her sweaty brow and threw the apron over her head.

"Take a breath, friend." Debbie set two empty glasses in a dish-washing tub beside the drink fountain. "It's been slow this morning, between the cold weather and people getting their lives back after the holidays. Charla is busy whipping up some chicken salad as a lunch special."

Janet took a moment to get her bearings before tying her apron. She was known for her ability to manage stressful situations without getting rattled, but after her experience with Kate, she could now empathize with every person she'd ever seen snap under pressure. "I'm so sorry about this morning. I thought I was just dropping off gingerbread."

"No explanation needed. If it involved Kate, I'm fully aware of the drill. Five years ago, I signed up for a Bible study at church, and the next thing I knew I was leading one of the discussion groups and organizing a coat drive for the local homeless shelter."

Janet adjusted her apron, still catching her breath after running from her car to the café. "Wait. How did you get from Bible study discussion group leader to coat drive?"

"Ah, but you forget, this was not your ordinary, everyday Bible study. It was a Kate Lipton Bible study, which always includes a little something extra. In this case, the something extra was a coat drive. For extra fun—"

"There's more?"

"Oh yes. Lots. Discussion group leaders were expected to be available for questions throughout the week, which sounded straightforward enough until some of those questions turned into late-night crisis-of-faith and what-did-I-do-to-make-my-teenage-daughter-hate-me calls."

Janet tried to recall Debbie sharing this experience with her when it happened. Nope. It was completely new information. "Why is this the first time I'm hearing this story?"

"I was most likely too busy collecting coats and reading parenting books to talk about it at the time. That being said, roping people in before they know the full scope of what they've signed up for is Kate Lipton's superpower."

"I got that impression." Janet took a clean glass off the rack behind her and poured herself a glass of water. "So I guess it won't shock you that she just added a published class anthology to her workshop. We spent the last ten minutes together brainstorming titles and came up with *Our Collective Memory*." She took a sip of water and let its coolness, along with the fragrance of cinnamon and apple wafting in from the kitchen, calm her soul. "That part was actually fun. Brainstorming with senior citizens is a hoot."

"See now, that's the good side of Kate's power to persuade. She has the energy of three people, and she's also creative, dynamic, and gets a lot done."

"I must admit it was fun to watch the class get excited about having their stories in a book." Now, how could she tell Janet that Kate expected to use her as a permanent class assistant? Then again, Debbie might be the perfect person to help her figure out how to get out of this predicament. "Speaking of Kate's power to persuade…"

"Let me guess. She's starting her own publishing company right here in Dennison, even though she would be slumming, and would like you to provide daily refreshments for her staff?"

"Not quite. But close." Janet took another sip of water. She slid onto the stool, facing Debbie. "She volunteered me as a class assistant, along with Roberta—the woman who left the note for Harry the other day."

"She was there too? How do they know each other? Did Kate see the poor woman outside the café and say, 'Hello, my name is Kate Lipton. Have I got an opportunity for you'?"

"They seemed to know each other pretty well. I have a feeling that Kate was the friend Roberta left to help yesterday."

Debbie chuckled. "This whole scenario is more dramatic than even I could imagine."

"This isn't funny. What happened to asking first? Or respecting a person's job?"

Debbie leaned her head back and laughed. "Sorry. I really am. I shouldn't be laughing about this. It's just so ridiculous. It might make sense for her to ask for your help with a baking class. But a writing workshop? It makes as much sense as moms texting me at midnight for advice on raising teen girls."

"Exactly." Janet put her elbows on the counter and dropped her head into hands. "To make matters worse, I thought I was helping out only for the day. But then I went and did such a great job that she's hoping I'll stay for the whole workshop. I want to support the class, but my mother got all the writing and editing genes, not me."

"You've written muffin recipes. Oh, and your now-famous gingerbread recipe. You also wrote that down."

Charla bustled out of the kitchen. "I'm eavesdropping, and I don't know whether to give this Kate Lipton a talking-to, or give you a big hug?"

Janet held out her arms in her best impression of a needy child.

Charla rushed over and wrapped her arms around Janet. "You poor thing."

"You're the best." Janet leaned into her friend's embrace. Then she sat back and composed herself. "I have no idea why Kate thinks I did a good job. All I did was write while Eileen dictated her story about taking over as stationmaster of the depot in 1943. Anyone could have done that. Of course, if I'd known that's what I'd be doing, I would've brought my laptop and saved my hand from cramping." She flexed her fingers. "Then we both spent the rest of the time trying to get Kate's grandmother to open up. Her challenge isn't the physical act of writing. It's being willing to share anything. She just looked at me like, 'You know I'm only here because my granddaughter dragged me, right?' Of course, Roberta drew stories out of people as if she does it for a living."

Debbie wet a cloth and started wiping the counter. "I really do feel bad about this, Janet. When I warned you not to let Kate talk you into anything, I was joking around. I never expected something like this. Seriously, you can say no to her. I don't think anyone ever has. That might be part of the problem."

Janet stood and tried to distract herself with something she excelled at. Muffins and pastries. She opened the bakery case to see what needed replenishing before customers started showing up for lunch. "Trust me, I rehearsed a great 'I need to decline' speech on the drive back here. But for some strange reason, I feel like I'm supposed to help. I feel extremely torn. Eileen was so excited to see me there. I enjoyed helping her. But I'm supposed to be here at the café in the mornings, not at Good Shepherd assisting with a workshop."

"You've got me," Charla shouted from the kitchen.

Debbie looked around the almost-empty dining room. "We were fine this morning. We also have Paulette. The question is, do you want to help Kate? It's one thing for her to ask for your assistance today, but assuming you'll be one of her sidekicks for the entire month is pretty presumptuous, in my opinion."

Janet pictured Harry dutifully writing in his red spiral note-book and recalled the tap of laptop keys and quiet conversations in the room. Roberta helped two women come up with ideas for their anthology contribution. By the time class ended, Janet and Eileen had managed to get Nora engaged in a conversation and found out that she once taught high school English and history. When she shared that her father died in World War II, Janet thought she'd finally found a starting point for helping her write a story. But by then it was time to brainstorm titles for the anthology.

Janet knew Kate appreciated having her there. With the exception of Nora, the others in the workshop seemed to enjoy every second of this opportunity to write about their lives. And the looks on their faces when Kate announced the anthology? If Janet pulled out, it might be harder for them to finish their stories in time. "I don't mind being her sidekick. I just wish she would have considered my job here."

She took her water glass to the kitchen and set it in the sink. "Are you sure you don't mind, Charla?"

"Not at all. I'm having a blast."

Janet and Charla went into the kitchen, where Janet opened the refrigerator to get the pot of split pea soup she'd prepared that morning before the café opened. "In that case, what do you say we get ready for the lunch crowd?"

Janet set the soup pot on the stove and reached for a long spoon. In the comfort of the café kitchen, with Charla beside her slicing onions for burgers and humming, she thought about the eager elderly writing students at Good Shepherd. And then there was Nora. Pulling stories out of her was like extracting teeth. But there was something about her. Janet sensed that Nora wanted to tell her story but didn't know where to begin.

Tamping down her frustration with the situation, Janet said to Charla, "Thanks for rescuing us."

Charla stopped midslice. "I'm happy to help out around here even if you want to say no to Kate."

Janet stirred her soup and listened to the chatter of more in-coming lunch customers coming in through the kitchen door. "It's only until the end of the month. Who knows? It might be fun to take on a new challenge that doesn't include flour and cookie cutters."

"You can do it for Harry."

"That's right. It's for Harry. And Eileen and Ray. They have incredible stories that need to be told. And I have a feeling Kate's grandmother does too."

# CHAPTER SEVEN

*April 14, 1945*

*Halfway through an early Saturday shift, Harry pushed an empty baggage cart across the platform. He spotted Birdie inside the waiting area of the depot writing in her notebook. She had her camera beside her on the bench and her arm looped through the strap. Her older sister huddled with two other teenage volunteers outside the door of the canteen. Harry had caught enough of the conversation to know Margaret managed to buy a lipstick with her pocket money and hide it from her mother and her friends helped her wipe it off before she went home. Harry shook his head. Girls.*

*Miss Eileen followed Harry into the waiting area. She was even kind enough to hold the door open while he pulled the baggage cart through.*

*"Thank you, Miss Eileen."*

"You're welcome." She held the door for an incoming passenger. "Harry, before you leave for your lunch break, I have a favor to ask."

"Sure thing." Harry pushed the cart into the corner beside the ticket booth.

"A new mechanic is due to arrive any minute to help with the repairs and maintenance on some of the freight cars. I need to check on the status of the next train, so would you mind showing her to the maintenance yard? She's only lived in Dennison for a few weeks, so she isn't familiar with the station."

"I'd be happy to."

"I appreciate it." Miss Eileen started heading toward the stationmaster's office then turned back around. "One more thing. If you notice a man in a red stocking cap hanging around the station, please let me know. A couple that came to see their son off this morning complained about the man panhandling. Someone else mentioned the same problem yesterday."

"I've seen him," Birdie said without looking up from her notebook. "He wanders all over town. I think he might be a drifter, but he never has a suitcase or sack with him, so it's possible he's just poor. I tried to ask his name once, but he wouldn't tell me."

Miss Eileen's eyes grew large with concern. "Birdie, I know you're a curious girl, but you shouldn't talk to strange men, or any strangers for that matter. Promise me you'll stay away from him from now on."

Birdie sighed and shut her notebook. "Yes, ma'am."

Miss Eileen continued on to her office.

Margaret threw open the door, letting in a flash of sunlight. "Birdie, come on. Mother wants us home for lunch. We have chores."

"Coming." Birdie put her camera around her neck and slipped her pencil into her pocket then headed to the door. "See you, Harry."

"See you, Birdie."

Barely a minute passed after saying goodbye to Birdie before Harry heard the front door of the depot swing open again. When he turned around, he saw a girl about his age standing beside the map showing all the train routes. She wore a mechanic's uniform and had a toolbox in one hand. She flashed a beautiful smile when she noticed Harry standing there. Her teeth were white and straight, as if they were from a magazine toothpaste advertisement. He'd seen her before, but her name escaped him. He fumbled for words and finally managed, "Are you the new mechanic?"

"I sure am." She held her arms out. "You're not imagining things. I'm a girl."

"But..." She was too young to be a mechanic, wasn't she?

"Don't look so surprised. All the other women are doing their part while the men are off fighting. Why not me?" She raised her toolbox like a prized possession. "I just finished training. So, where are the freight cars that need tending to?"

"They're in the maintenance yard." Harry motioned for her to follow him as what felt like a cloud of bats flew around in his stomach. "Out back."

"I've seen you at church and school," the girl said.

That's why she looks familiar. *He'd seen her in the choir on Sunday, and a few times in the hall between classes. She was new in town but already had a group of girls to eat lunch with.* "That's right. I've seen you too."

"Aren't you going to introduce yourself?" She stepped to the side while he opened the door leading to the maintenance yard. "If we're going to work at the same depot and attend the same church and school, we ought to at least know each other's names."

Harry let go of the door handle, his eyes fixed on the girl's smooth skin and her eyes so full of life. "Oh yeah, sorry. My name's Harry Franklin. What's yours?"

"Sylvia. Sylvia McCurdy." She held out her hand. "I just moved to Dennison two weeks ago, from Columbus."

"Nice to meet you, Sylvia." His palm was sweaty, so he quickly wiped it on his jacket before holding out his hand.

She shook it with a grip as firm as any boy's, but her skin felt baby-cheek soft. "Nice to meet you too, Harry."

He gripped the door handle again. "So, I just have to ask. How old are you?"

"Sixteen."

"And you're a train mechanic already?" He cocked his head. "I don't know of any sixteen-year-old-girl train mechanics."

"You don't look much older than I am, and you work here."

"Yes, but I'm just a porter." He'd started working at Dennison Station when he turned fifteen and already had his sights set on being a conductor someday.

Sylvia smiled again. Harry's heart went back to fluttering, in a way he'd never felt before.

"Don't you worry," she said. "I'm here to meet my aunt." She even said aunt the proper way instead of pronouncing it the same way as the insect. "Aunt Marion took over her husband's job with the railroad. He's overseas fighting in the Pacific. My father is over-seas too, in Europe. My mom and I just moved in with

Aunt Marion to share expenses. Starting today, I help out on Saturdays and after school when I don't have too much homework."

Something about Sylvia's confidence made Harry want to know her better. She didn't seem like the type of girl to buy forbidden lipstick and stand around flirting with servicemen at the canteen like Birdie's sister.

Harry held the door open for her. "I think it's wonderful that you're a mechanic. My mother works in the laundry at Fletcher General Hospital."

"See, we're all finding ways to use our talents while our men fight."

Harry ran out of words. He didn't realize he was standing frozen at the sight of Sylvia's pretty face until she waved her toolbox through the open door. "So, is the maintenance yard that way, or..."

Harry startled. He cleared his throat and squared his shoulders. "Yes, it is." While leading the way to the yard, he predicted what Birdie would write in her composition book if she hadn't gone home already. I believe Harry Franklin found a sweetheart today.

# CHAPTER EIGHT

en minutes after Debbie sent Paulette home early, the café went from almost empty to filled with locals coming in for hot drinks, cups of soup, and pastries. Janet was spraying whipped cream on a slice of apple pie for a new customer who'd heard good things about the Whistle Stop when she saw the owner of Aunt Maggie's Antiques and Consignment walk in.

Janet waved to her. "Hello, Anne. It's nice to see you."

Anne came over to the bakery counter. "After meeting you at my store the other day, I started craving your gingerbread. I left my husband in charge for a while with the promise that I'd bring some back for him."

"You're in luck. I just sliced a fresh loaf. I added some drizzle icing this time. It was a hit with a group I served this morning, but you can be my quality-control inspector and tell me if I should use the icing or stick to plain powdered sugar."

Anne closed her eyes and sniffed the air. "I can smell it through the glass. I'm happy to be your quality-control inspector anytime." She pulled out her wallet. "I'll take two slices to go."

Janet pointed to one of the stools along the counter. "Have a seat while I box it up for you." She put the apple pie on a tray and set it aside for Debbie to serve. "Did you see what I did with the lap desk and pen?"

"Yes. I was just admiring it. I can't wait to add a note to your board on my way out." She swiveled around for another look. "My aunt Maggie would approve, for sure."

Anne set her purse on the next stool over. "My husband was a little upset with me when he found out I sold that fountain pen without waiting for him to research the value first. I'd taken a picture of it, and the desk, before putting the items out for sale—you know, for inventory purposes. Then I entered the descriptions into our inventory book. When Rick saw the unusual color, he looked it up and discovered Parker only released a few of them, in 1932. After seeing that I let it go for fifteen dollars, he was not happy."

Janet opened her mouth to offer to return the pen, but before she could get a word out, Anne waved her hand. "Now, don't worry about it. I reminded him that the pen belonged to *my* great-aunt, so technically, I could give it away if I wanted to. He couldn't argue with that. Not for long anyway. Besides, I don't know if you saw it, but we have a sign in the shop that says 'All sales are final.' That goes both ways, so I'm just happy it went to someone who's sharing it."

*Thank You, God.* "I'm so glad," Janet said. "It's been a hit around here." Such a hit that when she considered putting it away and only taking it out for Harry, she'd talked herself out of it.

"I'll be sure to tell my husband. He'll appreciate knowing something good came out of my mistake. We figure once we put a price on something, if we missed the true value of the item, it's on us. It just goes with the territory."

Janet opened the bakery case and zeroed in on two thick slices of gingerbread. "Can I get you some coffee to go with your snack?"

Anne looked over her shoulder at the writing station. "Two cups of black tea would be great. Thanks. I wish I could stay. But I have a couple of errands to run before relieving my husband."

Janet handed the bag to Anne and slid cardboard sleeves around her to-go cups. "Please come back again soon."

"I look forward to it." Anne handed over some folded bills. "No need for change." She took her bag and held up her cups as if giving a toast. "Gotta run."

Janet watched her stop at the writing station to make use of the old fountain pen. Before pinning her note to the board, Anne came back and showed it to Janet.

*Be willing to give something valuable away. You never know who might need it.*

"I love it," Janet said.

Anne grinned, hurried back to the message board, tacked her note up, and picked up her cups and bag. Janet was wondering how she'd navigate opening the door, but just as Anne got to it, Harry arrived with Crosby and held it for her.

She thanked him, and he wished her a good afternoon.

Harry unzipped his coat. "Do you ladies mind if I hang out for a while and do some writing? I'm having a bit of writer's block."

Debbie raced past him with two mugs of hot chocolate. "Not at all."

He picked up the fountain pen. "Is it okay if I use this? I'm working on my pen story and thought it might help."

Seeing how seriously Harry was taking the writing class confirmed Janet's decision to continue helping Kate with the class. "Go for it, Harry."

He found a chair near the counter. "I read that a lot of authors do their best writing in coffee shops, so I figured I'd give it a go."

Debbie set a cup of coffee in front of him. "This will complete the look and get your creativity flowing. It's on me."

Harry opened the pen and his red spiral notebook. "Why, thank you, ma'am."

While Janet and Debbie busied themselves with customers, Harry sat writing and sipping his coffee as if he were the only person in the café. Crosby snoozed at his feet. Occasionally Harry stopped to examine the pen in his hand and got a faraway look in his eyes. Janet longed to casually walk behind him to offer a coffee warm-up and peek over his shoulder, but his comment about trying to overcome writer's block kept her behind the counter where she belonged.

A young mom and her preschool-aged daughter walked into the café. Janet recognized the pair from when they came into the café with the rest of their family just before riding the Christmas train in December. The little girl wore the same red sparkly snowflake sweater she'd worn for the train ride, this time with orange polka-dot leggings, a pink coat, and purple snow boots. She stomped her feet on the door mat then ran over to the bakery case. Her mom caught up with her and took her hand.

Janet leaned over the counter. "What would you like, sweetie?"

The little girl's mom squatted down. "Tell her what you want, Tabatha."

"Hot choc-lit, please."

For the mother's sake, Janet restrained herself from asking the child if she chose her own outfit that morning. Clothing battles that ended with her letting Tiffany face the social consequences of going to school looking like a clown were still fresh in her mind. "It's a hot chocolate sort of afternoon, isn't it?"

"Uh-huh."

"I'll have a latte." Tabatha's mom took out her wallet.

While Debbie prepared the hot chocolate, Kate came into the café, sending a current of trepidation through Janet's entire body. *Please, Lord, I can't say yes to another request.* She was surprised to see Nora come in behind Kate, bundled head to toe and pushing her walker. Janet let Debbie seat the pair and kept her attention centered on the cute little girl and her mom.

Tabatha ventured over to Harry and Crosby.

Harry stopped writing. "Well, hello there. What's your name?"

"Tabatha."

"It's a pleasure to meet you, Tabatha. I'm Harry."

Tabatha said hi to Harry and looked down at Crosby. "I have a dog."

"Do you now? What's your dog's name?"

"Bruno."

"Bruno's a nice name. This is Crosby. He's friendly. You can pet him if your mom says it's okay."

Tabatha's mother said, "It's fine, honey. Just be gentle."

The little girl knelt on the floor and stroked Crosby's back.

Harry went back to writing. Janet watched Tabatha split her attention between the white dog with the black spot over his eye and Harry. She stood up and pointed to Harry's pen. "What's that?"

"It's called a fountain pen."

"Fountains are for water."

"You're right about that. They are for water." He held out the pen. "But you see, in this kind of pen, the ink flows out through this nib here at the end, kind of like a fountain."

Tabatha reached for it, but her mom took hold of her hand.

"Want to try it out?" Harry asked her.

Her mother pulled out a chair. "What do you say?"

"Yes, please."

The next thing Janet knew, Harry had torn a page out of his notebook and was standing behind the little girl.

"Be very gentle, okay?" Harry gave her a little demonstration.

"I will."

He handed it to her.

Janet caught a glimpse of Kate, who looked ready to jump up from her table and snatch the pen out of Tabatha's hand. Instead, she waved Debbie over and said something to her quietly.

Debbie glanced at Harry and Tabatha. "It's fine," she said loudly enough for Janet to hear. "Harry is watching her."

"No, it's not. She's way too little to—"

"Don't go turning a two into a ten, Kate," Nora said from behind her menu. "Whatever you're stressing about, relax. Your blood pressure is high enough right now."

Janet almost gave Nora a thumbs-up from across the room. *I don't know whether to thank you, feel bad for Kate's inability to relax, or both.*

After a few minutes, Harry gently took the pen out of Tabatha's hand. "You did good." He praised Tabatha for trying so hard with something new then said, "Tell you what. How about you go to that desk over there and add a flower or two to those nice lines you just made. Then you can have your mom help you pin it to Miss Janet's special board. We have a lot of words up there, but I don't see any flowers."

"Okay." Tabatha slid off the chair with her paper.

Harry sat back down, and Tabatha's mom said to him, "That was so sweet of you."

Janet expected Harry to start writing his story again. Instead, he stared at the fountain pen. He replaced the cap and held the pen with both hands as if memorizing every detail of it. He opened his jacket and slipped the pen into the breast pocket of his red flannel shirt. He gave his pocket a gentle pat then took the pen out again and went back to writing.

Kate walked up behind him. "I see you're working hard, Harry."

"Yep. I thought it might be quiet in here today, but seeing all these nice people is inspiring in a different way."

Crosby sat up and stretched.

Kate looked down at the dog. "Well, I don't want to keep you from your creative process."

"See you Monday in class." Harry got busy again.

Kate paused for a moment and watched Harry write. Even as she walked over to the bakery case, her eyes lingered on him.

"Can I get something for you, Kate?" Janet asked.

Kate's eyes shifted as if she was jolted out of deep thought. She adjusted her sweater and tucked her hair behind her ears. "I just came over to apologize for this morning. I've been feeling terrible for putting you on the spot like I did. It was completely inappropriate of me."

"I appreciate the apology, Kate, thank you."

Kate's eyes drifted back to Harry.

Determined to let Harry write without being stared at, Janet said, "It will be fun to do something different."

"I owe you."

Janet noticed Kate's grandmother eyeing the writing station. Nora boosted herself up with the help of her walker and shuffled across the room to the desk.

"So, Nora," Janet called to her from the bakery counter, "did you decide what to write about for the anthology?"

She lowered herself into the chair. "I might've come up with something."

"Cool. What?"

"You'll have to wait until Monday, missy."

Kate's face turned red. "Gran. You can be so snarky sometimes."

Nora opened the writing desk. "Janet knows I'm just giving her a hard time."

Janet gave Kate a reassuring smile. "It's okay. She's right. A writer can't give away too much too soon."

Nora pointed to Janet, her eyes on her granddaughter. "See, she gets me."

"Well, I certainly try to." Janet watched Harry prop up his notebook to read a page. "Kate, are you two here for lunch, or just coffee and a pastry?"

"We came in for tea and a snack, but it was really an excuse to stop by to talk to you and Debbie."

Debbie looked up from filling the coffee maker, and Janet could see the *Oh no* look in her eyes.

Janet kept her eyes on the door to check for incoming customers. Debbie came over and folded her hands on the counter. "So, Kate, what can we do for you? And no, sorry, we can't hold the workshop here at the café."

Janet fought to keep a straight face. *Go, Debbie. Way to have some boundaries.*

Kate reached across the counter and nudged Debbie. "You are so cute. I would never ask you to do that. But I do have an idea that involves the café."

Janet managed to maintain a friendly expression.

The look on Debbie's face as she filled hot-water kettles for Kate's and Nora's tea told Janet that she was losing her sense of humor by the second. Debbie grabbed two mugs and set them down, probably harder than she meant to. "What's your idea?"

Kate sat on the counter stool closest to her. "It occurred to me after announcing the anthology that when a book is released, the author usually has a launch party with a signing. None of our workshop participants will become bestselling authors, but I do want them to feel like their stories are valuable. So I want to have a party to celebrate *Our Collective Memory*."

Harry's presence boosted Janet's enthusiasm for the idea. How many of Kate's students would ever have the opportunity to participate in a launch party for a book they contributed to? For some, it might even be a dream come true. "The class will love it."

Kate's face lit up. "I'm picturing fancy table settings and encouraging everyone to dress up and invite a guest or two. I'll bring in a local published author as a surprise guest speaker."

Janet racked her brain for names of published authors in the area. Surely there had to be some, but none came to mind. "I wish I could help you come up with a speaker. That's not my circle of influence."

"I already booked one."

How was that possible? Kate lived in Cleveland. And she'd just announced the idea for the book a few hours ago.

Debbie put the mugs and miniature kettles on a tray. "The party sounds like fun. I'm sure Good Shepherd will allow you to have a celebration meal if you ask right away. I don't know how formal they can make it, and it might end up being a brunch during the usual workshop hour, but—"

"Oh, I don't want to have it at Good Shepherd." Kate said it as if Debbie had just suggested having the party at the tackiest fast-food joint in Ohio.

Debbie reached for a basket of tea bags. "What do you have in mind?"

Janet had to give it to Debbie. She was making Kate spell it out.

"I'm hoping to have the launch party here, at the café."

Janet looked over Kate's shoulder at the rows of square tables topped with checked tablecloths, sugar jars, and ketchup bottles. "Here?"

Debbie's mouth quivered like she might be fighting the urge to say something sarcastic. Instead, she cleared her throat and said, "I don't know, Kate. We've had some events here, but nothing overly fancy. Our café isn't exactly a white tablecloth and candles sort of place." She waved her hand at the chalkboard behind her.

"Notice that our lunch special for today is grilled ham and cheese with a choice of fries or house salad. When we really want to switch things up, we serve our soda and iced tea in mason jars."

Kate went to the nearest table and stood behind it. "But we could easily make the place look more presentable." She started waving her arms like a flight attendant giving the safety talk. "We could switch out your checked tablecloths with white, bring in some candles and flowers, maybe string some light along the walls..."

Janet glanced at Debbie out of the corner of her eye. Debbie's brown eyes screamed, *What does she mean, more presentable?*

Harry watched the scene from over his reading glasses.

Kate nodded in the direction of the writing station, where Nora attached her note to the corkboard. "We could move all that stuff and set out copies of the anthology for family members to buy if they want an extra copy."

Janet's lips lightened. *That* stuff? Why ask to have her dinner at the café if she didn't like the look of it?

Before Janet could think of a gracious way to suggest she find another location, Debbie jumped in. "It sounds like a really nice idea, Kate, but Janet and I will need to talk about it and get back to you."

"Oh, of course." She held her hands up. "Definitely discuss it. Having an event like this might be good for business. Just sayin'."

Did she think they were struggling?

Nora got up and pushed her walker back to their table. "You might be able to sell them on the idea if you leave their nice place alone, Kate. Not everything needs to be fancy schmancy."

"I want it to be nice, Gran." Kate smoothed the tablecloth in front of her. "Maybe we can compromise. Checked tablecloths wouldn't be *too* bad."

Debbie took their tea to their table. "That might be possible, but I'd still like to think about it before I commit. Transforming the café for a dinner, formal or not, will take some planning."

Kate smiled. "I understand completely."

Debbie pulled out Kate's chair. "We'll get back to you by the end of the week. I promise."

Kate took a deep breath and returned to her table. "I appreciate you considering the idea."

Janet barely had time to recover from Kate's request when Roberta came in, saw Kate and Nora, and joined them for tea.

Janet kept her voice as low as possible while suggesting to Debbie, "Maybe we should move the class to the café. Considering how many participants are here already."

Debbie whispered back, "Don't even joke about a thing like that."

Before Janet could come up with a snappy wisecrack, she noticed an abrupt change in Harry's demeanor. Instead of writing, he stared blankly down at his notebook. Roberta got up from her chair and walked over to his table.

"How's your story coming along, Harry?"

"It's going all right."

Crosby got up and started pacing.

Janet went into the kitchen to get a cup of soup for another customer, and when she returned, Harry was almost out the door. "Goodbye, Harry," she called. "Happy writing."

"Thanks," she heard as the door closed behind him.

Janet noted how Harry's shoulders slumped on his way out. She told Debbie, "I'll be right back."

She caught up with him before he left the depot. "Hey, Harry, can I ask you something?"

"Of course you can. What's on your mind?"

Crosby watched Janet as if he also wanted to know what was on her mind.

"Does knowing Roberta wrote that nice note to you make you feel funny around her now? I feel bad for teasing you the other day."

"There's no need to feel bad, Janet. I know you were just joking around."

"I think she's trying to get to know you."

Harry looked around and came a little closer. "That's the thing, Janet. I think I know her already. And if she's the same Roberta I used to know, I don't know why she'd want to talk to me now."

Before Janet could remind Harry that someone who didn't want to talk to him wouldn't refer to him as an inspiration, Harry said a melancholy, "See you tomorrow," and walked away.

Janet locked the café door and flipped the sign to Closed. "What a day. I wonder how Ian will feel about ordering a pizza from Buona Vita for dinner."

"Sounds good to me." Debbie pulled off her apron. "Usually, I'd be thrilled about the rush we had just now, but when Kate and her grandmother came in, my stress level went through the roof. Then there was Harry, our light in the madness."

Janet was tempted to tell Debbie about the conversation she had with him after he left but sensed he'd said what he did in confidence. Instead, she sat in the chair beside the writing desk and brought up a moment involving Harry that Debbie had been part of. "That conversation between him and Tabatha—I wish we could've taken a video."

"It was darling. I had no idea he was so good with kids. I bet he was the sweetest grandfather."

"I can't wait to see his face when I give him the fountain pen. When I do, I might also give him the picture she drew." Janet stood to see what Tabatha had added to the lines she'd drawn with Harry. She immediately spotted Tabatha's fountain pen creation. Above each black line she'd made with Harry's guidance, she'd drawn circles and dots with purple gel pen that vaguely resembled flowers, and green squiggles for leaves. "Now that is cute."

Right below Tabatha's picture was a card written in beautiful blue calligraphy.

*This is the day that the Lord has made. Let us rejoice and be glad in it. ~ Psalm 118:24*

Janet said, "I bet Tabatha's mom wrote that."

Debbie grimaced and tapped a note in the bottom left corner. "Who do you think wrote that one?"

*Make the most of today. You never know what life will throw at you tomorrow.*

Janet's heart sank a little. "For some reason, I have a feeling Nora wrote it."

"I have a feeling you're right. How sad. It's so…depressing."

"It is. But in case you haven't noticed, she isn't the happiest person."

"I noticed. When we attended church together in Cleveland, I knew Kate spent a lot of time coming here to care for her grandmother. But she never mentioned her being challenging."

Janet sat down at the counter. "Maybe she's just challenging now because of the adjustment to living at Good Shepherd and her back surgery being unsuccessful."

"Could be. Between you and me, Kate isn't acting like herself right now, so I have a feeling the adjustment is hard on her too. I mean, she's always been intense, but the last couple times I've seen her… I don't know how to explain it. Even the celebration dinner seems like an odd choice right now. You'd think she'd try to have less on her plate, not more."

Janet stretched her arms above her head and yawned. "So. What are we going to do about the launch party?"

Debbie crossed her arms and leaned against the counter. "I've been thinking about that for the last hour. If it didn't involve someone whose projects always become bigger than planned, I would say yes without hesitation." She stomped her foot. "Grr. I really want to do the dinner for Harry and the others."

"So do I." Janet swiveled back and forth on the stool. "We could always say yes to the dinner and no to making it formal. It's not like she's asking us to let her use the café at a time when we're serving other customers."

"We could." Debbie strolled to the closest table and fingered the checked tablecloth. "Or we could go all out and make it extra special for the seniors in this community who are taking time to write their stories. This is a terrible thing to think about, but we have no idea how much longer we'll have Harry and Eileen and Ray with us."

Janet considered that. She didn't even want to imagine the day when Harry would no longer be a daily fixture at the depot, either watching the trains from his favorite bench or sitting inside the café with Crosby, drinking coffee and visiting with locals. "You just sealed the deal for me. Let's host the dinner. No mason jars or checked tablecloths. We'll find white tablecloths and inexpensive candles and transform this place into a five-star restaurant." Between their mothers and Charla, they could borrow all the decorations.

"You mean a five-star restaurant with red and yellow walls and World War II memorabilia. Including our framed poster of Rosie the Riveter."

"Let's make that part of the charm. I bet we can even get Kim involved somehow."

Debbie nodded. "I'll ask Greg to be the maître d'. Maybe we can get him to wear a tux. Or at least a jacket and tie."

Janet's mind started spinning with fun possibilities. "Let's also ask his boys to be waiters, along with Paulette. Charla can help me in the kitchen. She'll love it."

"Yes!" Debbie put her hand up for a high five.

"I'll get Ian to help as well."

Debbie pulled her order pad out of her pocket and started jotting down notes. "While we're completely taking over Kate's dinner, I have another idea. To avoid the possibility of this becoming an overblown production where Kate invites media from the network news, how about if we tell her that all she needs to do is show up with her surprise guest speaker and copies of the anthology? We'll handle everything from the menu to the decorations."

"Now I'm even more excited."

"So am I." Debbie started reaching for her phone then put it back in her pocket. "Let's hold off on telling her though. I still have mixed feelings about her showing up with such a big ask right after recruiting you for her class. It'll do her good to wait."

"Agreed. The next class isn't until Monday, so I'll give her a call tomorrow." Janet reread Nora's note. "I bet Nora will enjoy the dinner despite her 'fancy schmancy' comment. I know I just met her this morning, but I have a feeling she's the one who needs a party the most. If I suddenly had to move into assisted living, I'd be crabby too. Like Eileen said today, she likes to talk tough. But I sense it's all an act."

"Or she had to toughen up for a reason." Debbie went over to the register and locked it. "Now for the big guessing game. Who will Kate's local author turn out to be?"

"Hey, maybe it's Harry and he's been writing under a pen name all these years." Janet opened the writing desk and straightened the stacks of paper and cards.

"I'll be in the kitchen tidying up."

"I'll give you a hand in a minute. I just need to put the fountain pen to bed for the day."

"Then we can add to our 'Who Is the Mystery Author' predictions."

"If it's not Harry, maybe it's Kim." Janet reached over to pick up the pen box. It seemed too light. She opened the box, and her heart sank.

# CHAPTER NINE

*D*ebbie!" Janet pulled back the chair and searched under the table. She opened the lap desk to see if someone put the fountain pen inside after writing a note instead of returning it to the box. It wasn't there or in any of the drawers or inside the inkwell slot with the other pens. "Can you come out here, please?"

Debbie came hurrying out of the kitchen. "Is everything okay?"

"Did you happen to move the fountain pen?"

"No."

Janet's heart raced. "It's gone."

"Are you sure?"

She lifted the lap desk and tipped it forward, hoping to see the marbled copper beauty roll out from under a stack of stationery. "Yes. I've looked all over the desk, under it, behind it." She peeked under the chair. "Where did it go?"

Debbie joined the search. She lifted the mat by the café entrance and then started searching under the tables. Janet extended her quest to behind the cash register and even unlocked the door and started looking around the café entrance inside the depot. She ventured over to the benches where passengers used to wait for trains, and even to Kim's museum ticket office with the tribute to Bing the War Dog. "This can't be happening."

Kate's scolding voice taunted her. *I warned you.*

Janet dragged her feet back to the row of benches and sank onto the one facing the ticket office, wanting to cry.

Debbie came out and sat beside her. "We might have more luck in the morning. It's pretty dreary outside right now, so the light isn't the best."

Janet reached into her pocket and pulled out the empty wooden box that had held the old Parker Duofold. "You don't think someone took it, do you?"

Debbie shrugged. "I can't think of anyone who came in today that I'd suspect as a thief."

Janet let the empty box drop into her lap and lowered her face into her hands. "Kate was right." She glanced between her fingers at the box then covered her face again and groaned.

Debbie scooted closer and rested her hand on Janet's back. "Hey. Try not to jump to conclusions, okay? It could still be around here somewhere."

Janet dropped her hands. "But where? It isn't anyplace that makes sense."

Debbie stood up and put her hands on her waist. "Harry used it today. Maybe he borrowed it to finish his story at home."

"He wouldn't take it home without asking one of us first. Unless he took it by mistake in his hurry to leave."

"Maybe he did." Debbie started pacing and stopped at the front window of the café. "Who else was here at that time?"

If the pen had disappeared the day before, counting customers would be easy. But the afternoon had gotten so busy that Janet had to think. "Anne from the antique store, that little girl and her mom, Kate, Nora, Roberta, and then the many random people who stopped in for coffee and pastries."

"Do you think the little girl wandered off with it?"

"No. After Harry let her try it out, he took it back and encouraged her to draw the flowers she made with that purple gel pen."

"That's right."

"Anne wrote a note with it. But that was before Harry came." Janet looked at the empty box again. She remembered Anne's comment about her husband being upset with her for selling the pen for such a low price. Could he have been one of the new customers who came in for coffee? She wouldn't recognize him if he did.

Debbie patted Janet's knee. "Don't worry. We'll find it. Someone must have seen what happened to it."

Janet led the way inside. She dragged her feet to where she kept her tote bag, and dropped the empty box into it. "Someone probably took it by mistake. At least I hope that's what happened."

Janet was sprawled on the couch with her big gray cat on her chest when Ian came through the front door. Laddie, their Yorkie, barked like a guard dog ten times his size.

"Hey, tough guy," she heard Ian say. "Where's Janet, huh?"

"I'm in the living room." She hadn't even thought about dinner let alone started anything. Even ordering pizza felt like too much of a chore after the day she'd had. A World War II romance that Debbie gave her for Christmas lay across her knees, waiting for her to get through more than a page, even though she loved everything about the book. She picked it up to see who the author was. Elsie James. She made a mental note to look for more of her books.

Janet stroked Ranger's silky fur. She tossed her book onto the coffee table, making the cat jump.

When Ian came into the living room, he stood at the foot of the couch and stared down at her. "Are you okay? You look upset."

She sat up and moved her feet to the floor to make room for her husband. "Not really."

Ian gave her a kiss and sat beside her on the couch. Laddie joined them. "You aren't getting sick, are you? The holidays may be over, but the season for colds and flu is still upon us." His hint of a Scottish brogue came through as he spoke.

"No, I'm not sick. Not physically anyway." She leaned her head against the back of the couch and rubbed Laddie's ears. Where should she begin? The writing class and hosting a formal dinner felt like minor concerns compared to how her day at the café ended. "That nice fountain pen that we bought with the lap desk went missing this afternoon. One minute Harry was using it to write a story, and the next…" She snapped her fingers. "Poof."

"Oh no. I'm sorry, hon. Maybe it just rolled behind the desk."

Janet shook her head. "No. I looked. So did Debbie."

Ian yanked off his boots. "I might be thinking like a cop, but do you find it suspicious that it disappeared twenty-four hours after finding out that it's worth a lot more than what we paid for it?"

Janet closed her eyes. The same thought had nagged at her the whole way home. "A little. But who would take it? None of our regulars would steal from us."

"Unless it wasn't a regular. I know Dennison is a small town where everyone knows one another, but strangers do pass through. Did anyone new come into the café today?"

"We had a few new customers, but nobody who struck me as a petty thief. Close to the time when the pen disappeared, we served an older woman named Roberta, who has come in one other time. Kate Lipton came in with her grandmother. A woman came in with her little girl."

"Do you think it's possible that one of them took it?"

"Who would want to steal a fountain pen? Other than a collector."

"Criminals come in all shapes and sizes. They don't always look sketchy."

"*Lance would snatch this up in a heartbeat.*" Janet remembered the dreamy expression on Kate's face as she held the pen up to the light coming in through the café window the previous day. And then there was Debbie's comment about Kate not acting like herself. Did she… No, she wouldn't make two big requests and steal something from them on the same day.

*Would she?*

Ian tapped his fingers on the armrest of the couch. Ranger jumped off the coffee table. "It wouldn't have to be someone after a fancy fountain pen. For something like this, the thief is usually thinking of the money they can get from selling the item."

"But that would mean the person had to know the value of the pen, right? Besides, I didn't see anyone come in today who looked like they were in desperate need of money."

"But again, desperation isn't always obvious."

Janet recalled Kate's strong reaction to seeing Harry teach Tabatha how to use the fountain pen. As if a child wasn't worthy of trying it out with Harry and her mom right there to guide her. And then there was Roberta, who seemed to be showing up everywhere this week. And Harry's statement about her while leaving so suddenly. "Anything is possible at this point. We just need to find it." She sat up. "I was going to give the pen to Harry. He used to have one like it."

Ian wrapped his arm around Janet and pulled her close. "Well, unfortunately, a fountain pen probably won't land at the top of the priority list for a police investigation."

"Really? I was hoping you could pull some strings down at the station. Because this is an important pen."

"It is an important pen. It's important to you. You can report it as stolen property. It will help that you know the value."

"You're the absolute best. Do you know that?"

"I don't know about the *best*." Ian kissed the top of her head. "In addition to knowing the value, it will help if you have a picture of the pen and are prepared to describe any distinct details. Then if you see it for sale online somewhere, or in a pawn shop, you can dig deeper and press charges."

Janet considered what she had to go on when it came to reporting the value—a picture, the information Kim found for a pen that looked like hers, and Kate's story of what she saw one selling for in a store. "Kate Lipton's brother-in-law is a pen collector. He would probably know what I should list in a police report. But that would require involving Kate. I'd rather not risk an I-told-you-so lecture for leaving it out in the open."

"I don't blame you there."

Janet thought about Anne. "Anne from the consignment shop came into the café today and mentioned her husband being upset with her for selling the pen so cheap."

"Maybe he can help you. I know you said Kim showed you the value of a pen just like it. But to confirm that, you can ask Anne's husband how much he would have sold it for if his wife hadn't sold it to you first."

Janet nodded. "It's a place to start, at least. That won't get me any closer to finding it, but it'll help."

⚜

The next morning, Janet waited till after the breakfast crowd dispersed to drive to Aunt Maggie's Antiques and Consignment. She stood at the entrance, taking one deep breath after another before finally turning the doorknob. The cheery bells were a sharp contrast to the ache in her heart. She remembered when she asked to borrow a locket from her mom for '50s Day in seventh grade. Her mom had said no. She'd gotten it from her favorite aunt for her sixteenth birthday. But Janet sneaked it out of her mom's jewelry box and wore it anyway. It was so fun to show it off. Until she broke the chain while changing clothes for PE class. A friend tried to help her fix it, but after many attempts, Janet had to go home and hand her mom the broken necklace.

She hadn't borrowed the pen without permission. But she felt just as badly as she did all those years ago when she broke Mom's sweet sixteen locket.

She spotted Anne at the counter with a customer. Part of her hoped Anne's husband would be there to confirm the value of the pen while the other part didn't want to face the person who knew he could have gotten a lot of money for it.

*I need his help too much to worry about his reaction. God, please let him be as easy to deal with as his wife is.*

Janet spotted a slender salt-and-pepper-haired man in the room where she'd found the lap desk only days ago. She willed her heart to stop racing and focused on praying that this conversation would provide her with some answers.

"Hi, Janet." Anne's voice pulled Janet out of her thoughts. "Rick," she called, "Janet Shaw, from the Whistle Stop Café, is here."

Her husband came into the main room of the store. "So you're the one who might become responsible for post-holiday weight gain around here."

Janet held out her arms and then let them flop to her sides. "Guilty."

"What brings you back to the store?" Anne asked.

All Janet could manage was a dramatic sigh. *Just say it.* "I have some bad news."

"Oh no. What?"

Her husband came over to join them. "Is there something wrong with the desk you bought? If so, bring it in, and I'll be glad to take a look at it."

"I wish it was something that simple." Janet set her tote bag on the counter. "That fountain pen I bought from you?"

Anne picked up a beaded bracelet that someone had left on the counter and returned it to the jewelry basket. "Yes."

"It disappeared yesterday afternoon."

"Why didn't I see this coming?" Rick muttered.

"Rick," Anne admonished in a low voice.

Janet clutched the edge of the counter. "Debbie and I looked everywhere."

Rick let out a long, exasperated huff. "A rare fountain pen is not something that should be out with gel pens and ballpoints at a café."

Anne gave her husband a stern look. "Rick, it's not our pen anymore."

Rick put up his hands in retreat. "Janet, I apologize. It's just that as someone who deals with antiques, I don't like to see valuable items treated haphazardly. But Anne is right. What can we do for you?"

Janet closed her eyes and took a moment to calm herself. "I need to know the pen's value in case I want to report it as stolen property. Our museum curator found a fountain pen like it online, but I'd like to know the value of the one I bought from you."

Rick stepped behind the counter. "Anne took a picture of the pen for me before she sold it. Let me do a little digging." He opened a laptop and typed something. After a few minutes he said, "It was a Parker Duofold, 1932, in copper pearl, listed as rare."

"Correct."

He turned to Anne. "Who in your great-aunt's family owned something like this? They weren't wealthy."

She shrugged. "It was with Great-Aunt Maggie's things. I know it didn't belong to my grandmother. I asked Mom. It could have belonged to their other sister. Maybe it was a gift."

Rick ran his fingers through his hair. "Based on what I see in this picture, it was in good shape. If I had found this at an estate sale, or if someone brought it in to put on consignment, I would charge around eighteen hundred for it. I might not get that much, but I would consider that a fair price for a rare Parker Duofold from the 1930s. If you don't mind giving me your email address, I can write out a statement for you and send it this evening."

A giant wave of regret swept over Janet's heart. *I should never have set it out.* "I'll give you one of our cards."

At the same time, it hurt her to think someone might have taken it from the café.

Anne took Janet's hand like they'd been friends for years. "Don't beat yourself up, Janet. If someone stole the pen, then that person is to blame."

Rick shut the laptop. His face softened. "I truly am sorry for my reaction. You should be able to set something out in your own store no matter how valuable it is and trust that it will still be there at the end of the day."

Janet took a shaky breath. "I know that deep down. I just wish I knew what happened to it."

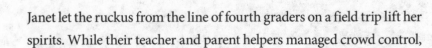

Janet let the ruckus from the line of fourth graders on a field trip lift her spirits. While their teacher and parent helpers managed crowd control,

Janet stood behind the bakery case with her tongs and a stack of paper bags to give each child a free cookie. She could see Harry through the window sitting on a bench in the warmth of the waiting area and letting the kids who'd already chosen their cookies pet Crosby.

A few boys and girls gathered at the writing desk. A tall girl pinned a card up with the word *Love* in bubble letters with a heart in place of the *O* while a freckle-faced boy moved the portable desk to his lap and selected a pen. Janet's stomach tightened. Now that the café was as busy as the day her fountain pen disappeared, the reality of the missing treasure hovered in a cloud of sadness. Seeing another boy drop a pen on the ground as he hurried to finish his creation reminded Janet how easily someone could have accidentally slipped the fountain pen into their pocket or tote bag. Unfortunately, it would have been just as easy for a dishonest person to steal it.

When the group of students left, the only cookies left in the bakery case were oatmeal-raisin and molasses, and the writing station was in serious need of some tidying up. Janet went over to replace pen caps and see what the children had pinned to the board. One student had drawn a cartoony likeness of Bing the War Dog. She was chuckling over it when Harry came in from his time of socializing with fourth graders.

"That was fun," he said. "I always enjoy it when school groups come to the station. I showed them a picture of me working as a porter when I was fifteen. Now they think I'm cool."

"That's because you are cool." Janet showed Harry the portrait of Bing.

Harry hunched down to talk to Crosby. "Look at that, boy. Your great-great-great-grandpa is a cartoon now."

Crosby wagged his tail and gave him a doggy smile.

"Too bad I don't have my notebook with me. I would try to do a little writing while I'm here."

Janet dropped her fistful of pens into the inkwell. This seemed as good a time as any to tell Harry. "I have bad news for you. Our favorite pen disappeared."

"How could it disappear?" He put his hands in his jacket pockets and turned them inside out before stuffing them back in again. "I hope I didn't take it home by mistake. I might've been the last one to use it yesterday."

"When you go home, would you mind checking the pockets of your shirt from yesterday, just in case?"

"No problem at all." A hint of sadness filled Harry's eyes as he looked over his shoulder to where the pen used to nestle in its box.

Debbie came out of the kitchen with something hidden behind her back. "In the meantime…" She smiled at Janet. "Close your eyes."

Janet put her hand over her eyes.

"She's gonna like that," Harry said a moment later.

"Okay, you can open them now."

When Janet opened her eyes, Debbie was holding a posterboard with a closeup of the beautiful fountain pen in the middle and LOST in giant letters above it.

HAVE YOU SEEN OUR FOUNTAIN PEN?
IF SO, PLEASE RETURN IT, NO QUESTIONS ASKED.
REWARD: BREAKFAST OR LUNCH FOR TWO AT THE CAFÉ, BAKERY
TREATS INCLUDED.

Janet studied the poster more closely to take in every detail. "Debbie, it's perfect."

Debbie set the poster aside and reached out to give Janet a hug. "I couldn't sleep last night and wanted to do something to help. Don't worry. We'll find it."

Janet pulled Harry into the group hug. "We will. We have to."

Harry patted her back. "If I find it at my place, I'll call you right away."

# CHAPTER TEN

*April 21, 1945*

*Harry tapped his fountain pen on his bedroom desk and reread the note in front of him one more time. He'd written it four times already and couldn't afford to waste any more paper.*

Dear Sylvia,

I would be honored to have you join me for the Youth Spring Picnic at Community Baptist Church.

Date – Sunday, April 29, 1945

Time – 1:00 p.m.

Picnic lunch provided.

Please RSVP at your convenience.

Sincerely,

Harry Franklin

*It was a bit formal. But asking a girl like Sylvia McCurdy out on a date called for formal language. With his stomach fluttering like it did every time he saw Sylvia, Harry checked the clock on his nightstand. If he didn't leave now, he would risk being late for his Saturday shift. He folded the note into fourths, picked up his fountain pen again, and wrote* Sylvia *in his neatest penmanship. He put the cap back on his pen, pulled on his jacket, and slipped the note and his pen into the inside breast pocket of his uniform.*

Lord, please let Sylvia say yes.

<hr />

*It was all Harry could do to focus on his duties that day. Even Birdie's chatter didn't keep him engaged. All he wanted to do was end his shift so he could walk out to the maintenance yard and give his invitation to Sylvia. Whether she said yes or no, he wanted to get the asking part over with. He and his brother, Lester, had agreed the night before that girls were so lucky. They got to be invited on dates instead of facing rejection by doing the asking.*

*When the five o'clock train pulled away from the station and Mitch, who was scheduled for the evening shift, stepped out on the platform, Harry tried not to appear too eager to leave and go find Sylvia. He held himself back from breaking into a run, waved to the other porter, and went to clock out for the day.*

*Miss Eileen followed him inside. "See you Monday, Harry."*

*He waved to her. "So long, Miss Eileen."*

*As soon as Harry filled out his time card, his heart started pounding with nerves. Here goes.*

*He exited the station and headed to the maintenance yard. From a distance, he saw Sylvia and her aunt Marion sitting on an open freight car, putting their tools away. He stopped and waited for them to finish and said another quick prayer.*

*Sylvia swept her hand in front of her, like she might be swatting a fly away, and scrunched up her face in a way that made Harry want to laugh. Even with her hair a little wild from a day of work and her uniform splotched with dirt and oil, Sylvia was the prettiest girl in Dennison.*

*Sylvia's aunt looked in Harry's direction then back at Sylvia. "You have a visitor."*

*Harry walked over to where they sat and greeted them.*

*Marion nudged Sylvia. "Go on. You're done for the day. Enjoy your visit. Then you get on home to wash up for supper."*

"See you there." Sylvia shut her toolbox and hopped down from the freight car. She waved Harry over. "Hey, you."

Her smile silenced the doubts racing through his mind that tried to convince him that a girl like Sylvia wouldn't want to go to the church youth picnic with Harry Franklin. "How are things coming along on this freight car?"

A look of pride shone in Sylvia's brown eyes. "Really well. Aunt Marion says it's almost ready for action. We're just waiting for a couple of parts. In the meantime, there are some others due for routine maintenance."

Sylvia said routine maintenance as if she'd been assisting her aunt for years instead of only a week. It was nice to see a girl so interested in trains and machinery. He'd overheard Miss Eileen say the war gave women a chance to show the world what they were made of. Seeing Sylvia clutching her toolbox in the same way that some girls would hold their handbag confirmed why he wanted so badly to take her to the picnic. Sylvia had substance as well as spirit.

He cleared his throat in preparation for what he'd really come to the maintenance yard for. "I have a question for you."

She raised her eyebrows.

*Harry reached into his pocket. "I thought I'd ask in a note." He held the folded page out. "Here you go."*

*Sylvia set her toolbox down and took the folded paper. Harry knew she'd seen her name when she gave him a sideways glance. She unfolded the page. That radiant smile of hers slowly spread across her face.*

*"Harry Franklin, you really know how to ask a girl out."*

*He felt his cheeks warm up.*

*She turned the note around. "It's even in ink."*

*Harry nodded. Only the best for Sylvia. He started reaching for his pen so he could tell her the story of how he got it, but this didn't seem like the time to be boastful. "So would you like to go to the picnic?"*

*Sylvia looked at the note one more time before tucking it in the pocket of her uniform. "I would love to go. I'll have to ask my mother. But if it's a church event, I'm sure she'll say yes."*

Thank You, Lord! *"I heard the minister will be there to lead us in a prayer time for the troops, if that helps."*

*"I'll be sure to mention that when I ask."*

*Harry felt like his feet barely touched the ground when he waved goodbye to Sylvia. He passed the canteen*

and saw two women lining a tray with sandwiches wrapped in wax paper. One of them turned to pick up a crate of apples, and the other went inside the canteen. Before he knew what happened, Harry saw the man in the red cap run around the side of the depot, dart past the table in front of the canteen, swipe a sandwich off the tray, and hide it under his threadbare coat.

Harry almost yelled, "Hey, you, put that back," but his voice caught in his throat. He looked around for Miss Eileen. She was nowhere in sight. The woman with the apples started filling a long, flat box, oblivious to what just happened. The other woman came out with a tray of cookies. Neither gave the sandwiches a second glance. Harry started walking toward the canteen to tell them someone stole from them, but stopped. Miss Eileen was the one he needed to tell.

Harry was planning how to break the news to the stationmaster when he saw the man squatting behind a garbage can, gobbling the sandwich so fast Harry worried he might choke on it.

What did it feel like to be that hungry?

Harry turned away in order to avoid humiliating the man by making eye contact with him. During the Depression, he'd seen many people go hungry, including some of his friends. But he could remember only one time when he'd been really hungry. Not the exaggerated, "Mama, I'm starving" that he thought might get him a snack an hour before supper, but really, truly hungry. It was Thanksgiving Day, and they'd gotten a flat tire on the drive to Grandma and Grandpa's house. He remembered how his stomach growled while he and Lester helped change the tire. He hadn't eaten since breakfast because his parents wanted him to save his appetite for turkey dinner. By the time they got to his grandparents' house, he felt nauseated with hunger. Now he felt embarrassed over considering that the day he learned what it felt like to starve. He'd only gone a few hours without food and had a big meal waiting for him. How long had it been since the man behind the trash can ate a full meal?

Harry's once light feet felt heavy. He heard the man in the red cap crumple the wrapping from his sandwich, shove it under the metal lid of the trash can, and run off. *I still better tell Miss Eileen. But when Harry reached the door of the depot, he couldn't erase the picture of a starving man cramming a sandwich into his mouth so fast that he probably didn't taste the bread or know what kind of filling was inside. It was too late for Miss Eileen to do anything anyway. The man had taken off.* Harry let go of the doorknob and turned to go home.

# CHAPTER ELEVEN

On Friday afternoon, Janet yawned and ran a cloth over the bakery case even though she'd already done it twice. She couldn't remember the last time she felt so grateful to close the café and go home to sit by the fire and read with Ranger on her lap and Laddie at her feet. The best part of the day had been watching regulars respond to the poster about the lost fountain pen by checking their pockets and purses and under tables.

When Debbie came over to erase the specials board, Janet revealed one of the reasons for her draggy demeanor. "I had weird dreams all night about searching the dark web for my fountain pen and hitting links that crashed my computer, my phone, and the whole system here at the café."

Debbie gave the board a final swipe with the eraser. "That's so bizarre. I had a dream last night that I stole the pen and felt so guilty about it that I stashed it in the dumpster out back."

Janet tossed her towel aside. "You didn't return it to me? You could have at least pretended to have found it under a table or something."

"No way. I was too afraid of you. You had Ian posted at the door to arrest whoever had stolen the pen and put them in jail for ten years, and I was about to get married."

"Who were you going to marry? Oh, wait, let me guess. Greg." It was getting pretty obvious that Debbie and Greg liked each other, even if neither wanted to admit it.

"No, I was not going to marry Greg." Debbie made a face reminiscent of the days when boys had cooties. "At least I don't think so. The guy kept changing. But I do remember the ring was gorgeous."

Janet stifled another yawn and untied her apron. "Is it horrible of me to be thankful that neither Kate nor Roberta came in today? I'm not ready for Kate's reaction to our sign."

"If it is, I'm also horrible. At least when it comes to Kate not coming in. She has a good heart, but as you discovered this week, she can be exhausting at times. But why Roberta? I thought you liked her because she left that sweet note for Harry?"

"I do like her. But I'm trying to figure her out. She's one of those people who, I don't know. She kind of lurks and observes. Something about her timing for showing up leaves me feeling like I'm an extra in a movie starring her, Harry, and Kate. Did you notice the change in Harry when she came in yesterday?"

Debbie set the eraser down and brushed chalk dust off her fingers. "I noticed he seemed unsettled, but I thought it was because we joked around about Roberta making eyes at him."

"I thought so too. But I think there's more to it. He acted weird when she came to help with Kate's workshop."

"Maybe they have a history."

All Janet could say without risking betraying Harry's confidence was, "I think they might." She hung up her apron and stretched her back. "For now, it's time to give someone a piece of good news.

Now that I've confessed my relief that Kate didn't come in today, I'm going to call her and tell her about the dinner."

"Good idea. You should go home and put your feet up after you make the call. I'll finish up in here."

Janet went to fetch her phone. "I think I'll take you up on that. My brain is a foggy mess today." She picked up her coat and tote bag and found her phone at the very bottom of her bag. "See you bright and early."

"Get some rest, dear friend."

Out in the waiting area, Janet spotted Harry standing by the window that faced the platform and tracks. To avoid disturbing him, she went to a corner of the depot that was hopefully out of ear-shot and pulled up Kate's number.

When Kate answered, her voice sounded strained, like maybe Janet had caught her at a bad time. "Hey, Kate, I just want to let you know that Debbie and I talked, and we would love to have the book launch party at the café."

"Oh, Janet, this means so much to me." When Janet heard the emotion in Kate's voice, she was even more grateful for the decision they'd made. "Thank you. How about if I stop by the café tomorrow so we can plan the menu and decor?"

Now for the speech she'd rehearsed in her mind in the middle of the night between alarming pen dreams. "Actually, Debbie and I would like to take this off your plate and make the decor a surprise. We'll come up with a menu idea and run it past you in a few days."

"But—"

"Trust me. Food is our specialty, and we know what our friends at Good Shepherd like to eat."

"I insist on paying for the food."

"I insist on keeping it affordable then. How about that?"

Janet could feel Kate's tension through the phone, as if the idea of not being in control of the dinner rattled her to the core. "We love the idea of encouraging people to dress up and invite family or a friend. But we want to make the menu and decor a surprise."

"I...I guess that would be okay." She paused. "I'm usually the one providing the surprises."

"This will be a whole new experience for you then." Janet walked to one of the benches to sit down. "Please let us do this."

"All right. I accept. Thank you, Janet."

"If I have any questions, I'll let you know."

"Oh, the theme!"

Janet sank back. *Let her have the theme.* "Do you have something special in mind?"

"I'm picturing something that reflects Harry, Eileen, and Roberta's generation. Maybe *Celebrating the Greatest Generation*? We could have big band music playing and servers dressed like waiters from a nice restaurant in the forties."

*Thank goodness for Kim's record collection.*

"That sounds like a fun idea. Music won't be a problem, for sure."

Kate responded with a breathy, "This is going to be good. Thank you again."

"We're looking forward to it." After ending her call with Kate, Janet sat still for a moment. January suddenly felt as hectic as the holidays, only in a different way. Harry had moved from the window to a bench, so she went over to sit with him before going to her car.

"How you doing, Harry?" She reached down to pet Crosby. "Hiya, boy."

Harry folded his hands in his lap. "I can't complain. Other than that, I checked the pockets of my shirt from Wednesday, along with my pants pockets, my coat, and everything else I could think of and didn't find the pen. I'm sorry."

"You don't need to be sorry. I'm grateful that you looked." It saddened Janet to see Harry looking so down. "How's the writing coming along?"

"I'm feeling a little stuck at the moment. I wrote the fountain pen story. But another one keeps coming to mind for the anthology. I'm just not sure I can write it."

"Since I'm part of the class now, maybe I can help you. What's it about?"

"It's about a girl who used to hang around this station during the war. She came with her sister, who volunteered at the canteen. Birdie couldn't have been more than ten or eleven, but she was really bright. I remember she wanted to be a writer, so much so that she wore a boy's blazer and messenger cap like a reporter. While her big sister—I think her name was Margaret—poured coffee and flirted with the soldiers, Birdie walked around with her composition book and camera and interviewed the soldiers as they stood in line for their sandwiches and doughnuts. I sometimes worried that the boys wouldn't appreciate being pestered, but they didn't mind at all. Maybe she reminded some of them of their kid sisters back home."

"That sounds like a great story." *Birdie and Margaret.* Why did those names seem significant?

"Between trains, she would follow me around, asking questions about my work, what I liked to do when I wasn't at the depot, if I had a sweetheart…"

"Did she become a writer?"

Harry looked down at his folded hands. "I don't know. One day she and her sister stopped showing up." He glanced at Janet out of the corner of his eye. "I've always felt bad about that. Because, you see, I think it might've been my fault." He turned his head away. "Actually, I know it was my fault. Partially, anyway."

Janet put her hand on Harry's arm. "What happened?" The expression on Harry's face stopped her. "Scratch that question. Maybe writing what happened could make you feel better. Even if you just write it for yourself and not for the anthology."

"Maybe it would." Crosby put his paw on Harry's knees. Harry cupped the pup's face and stroked his head. "It could be my way of telling Birdie I'm sorry."

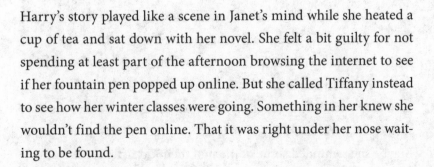

Harry's story played like a scene in Janet's mind while she heated a cup of tea and sat down with her novel. She felt a bit guilty for not spending at least part of the afternoon browsing the internet to see if her fountain pen popped up online. But she called Tiffany instead to see how her winter classes were going. Something in her knew she wouldn't find the pen online. That it was right under her nose waiting to be found.

# CHAPTER TWELVE

*April 28, 1945*

*Birdie perched on the edge of the bench and watched the long row of servicemen line up for sandwiches, cookies, fruit, and coffee at the canteen. They had fifteen minutes to take as much as they wanted before boarding the train. That morning, Mama had sent her and Maggie to the canteen with a bag of peanut butter and apricot jam sandwiches to donate. They were almost gone already. Paying attention to what each man chose was one of the interesting parts of tagging along with Maggie.*

*She wrote as quickly as she could.* The young man in the navy uniform took a sugar cookie and a shiny red apple and added them to his brown sack. Then he got in line for a sandwich. *Birdie slid off the platform, adjusted her messenger cap and old blue blazer*

*that her cousin Stanley outgrew years ago, straight-
ened the camera around her neck, and strutted toward
the man in the navy uniform.*

*"Hello, Sailor," she said to the tall, slender young
man. "Do you mind if I ask you a few questions? It'll
only take a minute."*

*"Not at all."*

*He had eyes the color of a robin's egg. She planned
to write that down.*

*"What's your name, and where are you from?"*

*"My name's Dave Stewart. I'm from Saint Louis."*

*She wrote his answer and the color of his eyes with
her stub of a pencil. John selected a sandwich and put
it into his brown bag.*

*"What kind of sandwich did you choose and why?"*

*"I chose ham because... Well, because they just ran
out of the other."*

*"You're lucky. Yesterday it was a choice of bologna
or plain cheese." She followed Dave to a stand stocked
with magazines, books, newspapers, and chewing
gum. "And what will you miss most when you're
overseas?"*

*"Hmm." He took the pack of chewing gum from
the box that Maggie held out to him and added it to his
bag. "My mom's fried chicken."*

*Birdie wrote* Mom's fried chicken. *The camera that her dad said she could borrow as long as she was careful hung like a medal of honor around her neck, making her feel like a real reporter. All she needed to feel official was a pen like Harry's instead of the old pencil and an eraser that smudged.*

*Maggie gave Dave a flirtatious wink.*

There she goes again. *Birdie cleared her throat to keep from groaning. Groaning during an interview would be unprofessional.*

*Maggie held out the copy of* Life *with Esther Williams on the cover.* "May I offer you a magazine?"

*"Thank you kindly." Dave smiled back at her. Before Maggie had a chance to turn on more of her charms, he stepped aside to make room for the man behind him in line.*

*Birdie had her next question for Dave Stewart at the tip of her tongue when he rolled up the magazine and said,* "Thanks for the interview, kid. Good luck with your report."

*Birdie let her arms drop to her side and gave him a half-hearted salute.* "Thanks. Have a safe trip."

*She heard Maggie tell the other girls at the table,* "I told her they all probably think she's doing a project for school. Whatever keeps her busy and out of my hair suits me just fine." Then she smiled and winked at the next man in line and offered him a magazine. "But if Mother knew about her talking to soldiers, she'd be in big trouble."

Birdie picked up a magazine and started flipping through it. "Not as much trouble as you'll be in if Mama finds out you wrote your name and address in this magazine."

Maggie yanked the magazine away from Birdie. When the next soldier came up, she slapped on another flirtatious smile. "Why don't you look for another soldier to interview, sweetie?"

"Okay, dear." Birdie let her sister go back to batting her eyelashes like a movie star. She knew Maggie only called her sweetie because she had an audience to impress.

She plopped herself down on the nearest bench to observe the men and women in line, those serving food, and all the other intriguing details that Maggie missed while being a flirt. When I turn fifteen, I won't behave like Maggie.

Birdie set her composition book on the bench and held up her camera to take a picture of Dave Stewart accepting a cup of coffee from one of the Salvation Army ladies, the magazine from Maggie rolled and tucked under his arm. At ten and a half, Birdie wasn't old enough to volunteer at the canteen, but she could still be part of the war effort by recording the soldiers' stories. Even if all she got were names, hometowns, and whether they liked ham or bologna, she could make up the rest. Someday, she would turn them into a book and become famous and Maggie would be sorry that she treated her so poorly.

Harry walked past her without saying hi. She would follow him if she didn't know he was busy with his responsibilities as a porter. So she took a picture of him looking so handsome in his uniform instead. He didn't even notice.

# CHAPTER THIRTEEN

On Sunday morning, Janet let her heart rest in the peace of church. Just as the service started, she saw Kate walk into the sanctuary and down the left side aisle with Roberta. While Ian folded his bulletin and put it in his Bible, Janet picked up her tote bag and dug through the side pocket as if desperately searching for a pen to take notes with. She silently asked God's forgiveness for wishing Kate and Roberta had chosen a different church to visit that morning, for this childish attempt to hide her face from them, and for being thankful that they arrived too late to come over to say hello if they did see her.

Instead of finding a pen, Janet rediscovered the business card she'd picked up during her first trip to Aunt Maggie's Antiques and Consignment. She'd forgotten to give it to Debbie. The worship team started playing an opening song, prompting the congregation to stand and join the singing. But Janet's mind wandered to the sight of Roberta and Kate three rows ahead.

*Birdie. That's a nickname for Roberta.* Was Harry's Birdie named Roberta?

And, according to Harry, Birdie had a sister named Margaret.

Did they call her Maggie, by any chance?

Janet tried to push aside the pieces of her current mental puzzle and concentrate on singing. But what she really wanted to do was slip out of the pew and drive to Aunt Maggie's to ask if Anne's great-aunt's "other sister" happened to be named Roberta, who went by Birdie as a child. If so, Harry's young friend from the train station sat only a few rows away from her.

If the missing fountain pen had truly belonged to Harry at one time, and Birdie was the person Harry gave it to, could she have decided she wanted it back?

Usually, Janet felt disappointed when Ian had to work on a Sunday, even after so many years of learning to accept it as part of being married to a member of law enforcement. As often as possible, especially when Tiffany was little, they tried to make Sunday afternoon a family time and do something together. But after spending the entire church service distracted by the names Birdie/Roberta and Margaret/Maggie and overanalyzing every encounter she'd had with Roberta over the past week, she welcomed the news that the police station was short-staffed because of a flu bug and Ian needed to go in right after lunch.

She gave him a kiss goodbye, cleaned up the mess from lunch, changed out of her church clothes into a cozy sweatshirt and jeans, and grabbed her tote bag for a drive a few miles north. She had checked online and saw that, like many shops in the area, Aunt Maggie's was open on the weekend and closed on Mondays.

Once again, the fragrance of cider and coffee greeted Janet as soon as she opened the door of the consignment shop. When Janet saw that Anne was busy with a customer and strolled over to the refreshments table, a sign posted on the wall behind it provided more warmth than the hot drinks offered.

HAVE YOU SEEN THIS FOUNTAIN PEN?

ONLINE?

IN A PAWN SHOP?

IN A CONSIGNMENT STORE?

IF SO, PLEASE CALL...

Like Debbie's poster, Anne's included an image of the fountain pen and a "No questions asked" reward—a $50 credit at Aunt Maggie's. The gesture of support brought such joy to Janet's heart that she no longer felt a need for coffee or cider.

She couldn't wait to thank Anne. The chatty customer was purchasing a stack of embroidered handkerchiefs and the teacup that Janet admired the day she came in with Ian for the first time. Janet strolled over to a display of framed vintage product ads and flipped through them to avoid hovering while Anne finished ringing up the woman's purchase. She listened as they finished their conversation about creative uses for the old hankies. By the time the customer left, Janet had taken pictures of three of the ads and sent them to Debbie for possible additions to the café.

"Welcome back." Anne adjusted one of the baskets on the counter then came around to the front and over to Janet. "Aren't those fun pictures? I can see the soft drink ad, with the soldiers looking through the train windows, in your café."

Janet held up the photo that Anne referred to. "I can too. I might just have to get it sometime." Though the soldiers looked a lot perkier than she imagined the average man felt when heading off to fight.

Anne took the framed print out of Janet's hand. "I'll hide it behind the others." She slid it between the last two prints and moved a cereal ad featuring Shirley Temple to the front.

"Anne, thank you so much for that sign you posted."

"I'm happy to do it. Any luck in your search for the pen?"

"No, unfortunately. But I think I have an idea of who owned it. Do you have a minute to talk?"

"Of course. Let me find Rick so he can mind the store while we visit." Anne went to a door marked EMPLOYEES ONLY and disappeared through it. When she opened it again, she waved Janet over. Janet passed Rick on her way and walked into a back room that had been the original home's kitchen and dining room. Anne and Rick had repurposed the kitchen into an office and break area, complete with two comfy chairs, a round table, and a meticulously organized corner desk. Janet peeked into the old dining area and found a long table with a set of labeled plastic drawers and a label maker in the center and shelves and plastic containers with inventory along one wall.

"I'm going to have some tea. Would you like a cup?" Anne's offer pulled Janet's attention back to the kitchen/office.

"I would love some. Thanks." Janet sat in one of the chairs by the round table.

Anne turned on an electric teakettle and brought over a tin of tea and two floral-print mugs. "This is a cinnamon spice tea that I got as a Christmas gift. If you'd rather have something else—"

"Cinnamon spice sounds delicious." Now that Janet was settled, she wasn't sure where to start when it came to her curiosity about

Aunt Maggie's possible connection to Roberta Daley. If there even was one.

"You won't regret it." Anne sat in the other chair. "So, what did you find out about the pen?"

"That's what I'm here to confirm. Did your aunt Maggie have a sister named Roberta?"

"She did. My grandmother, Ruby, was the oldest of the three. Then came Margaret, who went by Maggie, and Roberta."

"Did Roberta happen to go by Birdie?"

Anne pulled her sweater a little tighter around herself. "She went by that as a kid. Ruby—my mom's mom—passed away when I was a teenager, so it's been a while since I heard her stories of growing up. But I vividly remember her stories about Birdie. By the time I was born, Birdie went by Roberta." The teakettle whistled, and Anne got up to fill their mugs. "Grandma described her youngest sister as a precocious free spirit, but the affection in her voice gave away how much she adored her."

"I imagine that Birdie grew out of her free-spiritedness." Roberta appeared pretty sophisticated.

Anne set a steamy mug of hot water in front of Janet and nudged the tea tin toward her. "Yes and no. To me, she's always been my mother's cool mystery aunt who rarely attended family reunions, but when she did, she was the most interesting person in the room. She stood out with her pretty outfits and told stories about the people she met during her travels to England or Japan or wherever else she'd been that year."

"Your aunt Roberta has been coming to the café. She came in a few times last week."

Anne tore open a tea bag. "She's in town? The last time I saw her was at Aunt Maggie's memorial service last spring."

Janet realized how jarring it might be to discover that a family member came to the area without saying anything. "I'm sorry—"

"Don't be. It doesn't shock me. She's my great-aunt, so aside from me finding her fascinating, we aren't close. She moved to California ages ago. According to what I remember hearing from my mom, Aunt Roberta worked as a journalist. Her husband passed away suddenly when she was in her forties. She and her husband never had kids, and he left her well provided for, but she continued to work for her local paper and did some travel writing. I know Mom has always admired her for that." Anne removed the tea bag from her mug and set it on a plate. "So you think she owned the fountain pen, huh?"

"Possibly." Janet took a sip of her tea. The spiciness of the cinnamon and cloves awakened her senses. "One of our regulars at the café, Harry Franklin, used to own a pen just like the one I bought from you and mentioned giving it away a long time ago." How could she get the information she needed without sharing Harry's business in the process? "To make a long story short, a girl named Birdie who had a sister named Margaret came up in the conversation. Then I started connecting the dots and…" *And what? I thought I'd pop in to find out if your great-aunt is a thief? What am I doing here?* "I guess you could say I got curious."

Anne set down her mug. Her face lit up. "Do you want to see what else I found in the lap desk I sold you?"

"I would love to."

"I started looking through the stuff yesterday." Anne went over to the desk and took a flat box off the top of it. "Now that we're talking about Aunt Roberta, I'm sure what I found used to be hers. These are things that a budding journalist would have."

She returned to the table and set the box in the center. "My grandma Ruby was quite a bit older than Maggie and Birdie. See, now you have me calling her Birdie." She lifted the lid. "During World War II, Grandma Ruby served as a nurse in Japan. Her family lived in Dennison at the time. I remember her telling me that her sister Maggie volunteered at the Salvation Army canteen as a teenager. During one of the few get-togethers that all three sisters attended, Aunt Roberta teased Aunt Maggie about spending as much time flirting with servicemen as she spent passing out sandwiches. Maggie admitted it was true." She rummaged through the box. "I can't picture that at all. Aunt Maggie married a pastor and headed up a ministry for the homeless in Columbus."

Janet peered into the box. "I guess it's safe to say she grew out of her boy-crazy ways just like Birdie grew out of being a precocious little girl."

"Definitely." Anne took a plastic zipper bag out of the box. "The only item of value I found was the fountain pen. But there are some old pictures of the depot in here too."

Janet spotted a black-and-white composition book with a stain on the front. She picked it up and opened it. The name written in ink on the inside cover in youthful old-school penmanship felt like taking a step back in time. She held up the book and tapped the name *Birdie L. Cummings*. "Look."

Anne reached for the notebook. "Oh my goodness." She started flipping through the pages.

Janet took another sip of the comforting tea. "Harry told me that the Birdie he knew used to interview the soldiers at the train station."

Anne put her hand over her mouth and chuckled. "I think I'm reading one of those interviews right now. There's a description of Maggie flirting with a soldier, as Birdie put it, 'with the feminine wiles of Rita Hayworth.'" She flipped a few more pages. "It looks like she turned some of the interviews into stories. Some read like magazine articles and others like fiction." Anne handed the composition book back to Janet. "Check this one out."

Janet read the story titled, "Waiting." It was full of hokey dialogue between a soldier going off to war and a farm girl promising to be forever faithful to him. "I know I shouldn't laugh, but this is so cute."

Another page listed details about a young man name Dave Stewart. He wore a navy uniform and held a big red apple in one hand and a brown bag in the other. He was from Saint Louis and would miss his mom's fried chicken more than anything in the world. Birdie described couples parting after a final tearful embrace and boys thanking canteen volunteers for their generosity. Each page Janet turned included names and random details.

> *Name: Mark Howard, in the army*
> *Age: 19*
> *Has a girlfriend named Hazel with red curly hair. She thinks it's awful, but he thinks it's neat.*
> *Hopes the war ends soon so his kid brother doesn't have to enlist.*

Janet reminded herself why she'd come to the antique shop in the first place. To find out if Roberta and Birdie were the same person, so she could figure out if Roberta had a reason to take the fountain pen. She had no doubt that Roberta was Harry's Birdie, but with the young girl's composition book in her hand, she saw her as a thoughtful child who wrote about men who may or may not have returned from the war. "There's something so precious about what she did." She flipped to another page. "She turned the soldiers who came through Dennison into real people with names and favorite foods and girlfriends back home."

"If Aunt Roberta came into the store, I would give that book to her."

Janet saw a familiar name written in pencil. "Listen to this. It's about my friend Harry. It says, 'Harry Franklin is seventeen and has been working at the depot since he was fifteen. He doesn't have a sweetheart yet.' Then she wrote, 'I think Sylvia McCurdy, who helps repair engines, would be a perfect match for Harry. She is pretty and smart, and Harry acts funny whenever he looks at her.'" She closed the composition book and handed it back to Anne. "I guess Harry found his sweetheart. Sylvia was Harry's late wife's name."

Anne set the composition book aside. "This is like finding a time capsule." She opened the zipper bag. It contained black-and-white photos. She spread them out on the table and took another sip of tea.

Janet leaned over the pile. Most of them looked like they'd been taken at the depot. She recognized the canteen in candid shots of soldiers in army and navy uniforms reaching for sandwiches and holding out cups for volunteers to fill with coffee. She saw one of a man in a tattered coat and a woolen cap. He held a cup to his lips and was sitting on the edge of the station's platform. The next photo was of the same man, but this time he was glaring at the camera, his mouth twisted in anger.

*Now that looks like a man who would steal a pricy fountain pen.* The expression in his eyes was fierce. But he would be over a hundred years old by now.

The next picture in the stack triggered a cheerful gasp. "That's Harry as a teenager." The image was a little blurry, but she would recognize that friendly face anywhere. He was pushing a luggage cart across the platform.

Anne held another picture out. "Does this look familiar?"

It was a fountain pen on top of a composition book. Janet pulled the photo closer. Even in black-and-white, and a little blurred from age, she could make out the marbled design. She flipped it over and saw a faded caption. *Harry's fountain pen. He gave it to me on April 30, 1945.*

Janet held it up. "It's official. Your aunt was the friend Harry gave his pen to."

Anne rested her elbows on the table and stared at the picture. "I wonder what the story is behind that."

"This whole thing is so confusing. As soon as Harry heard your aunt's name and realized who she was, he started getting nervous around her."

Anne's eye twinkled. "Maybe she had a crush on him and left him little love notes written in her composition book. Harry gave her the pen as a bribe to leave him alone."

"Who knows? Maybe he did." Not that Janet could imagine Harry doing something like that.

Anne started returning the pictures to the plastic bag. "I wish this little dig could have gotten you closer to knowing what happened to your pen."

Janet took another look at the blurry black-and-white of Harry's pen. Birdie's pen. Her pen. A pen that had once belonged to a physician who gave it to Harry as a thank-you for returning his wallet. "It did help. Now I know it belonged to Harry, and to your great-aunt." She held up the photo. "Can I keep this?"

"Sure."

Janet slipped it into the inside zipper pocket of her tote, sensing that the answer to what happened to the fountain pen rested with one of its past owners.

# CHAPTER FOURTEEN

**B**efore Debbie opened the café the next morning, Janet transferred maple scones onto the same plate she'd used for the previous week's gingerbread. "I must be desperate to find out who took that pen," she told Debbie. "Last night I googled Roberta's name."

Debbie finished writing DENVER OMELET WITH HOME FRIES AND TOAST on the specials board. "Do you really think she had something to do with the pen disappearing? I just can't picture it." She added the price to the breakfast special. "I must admit, I find her interesting. Every time she comes in, she commands the room without saying a thing."

"I find her interesting too. But she was here when the pen disappeared and on the day that Kim told us how much it's worth." She pulled out a sheet of plastic wrap.

"So what did you find out from googling her?"

"Nothing. She isn't on social media." Janet laid the plastic over her scones. "I used her maiden name, Cummings, and her married name, Daley." She spun her plate, tightening the plastic as she circled around. "Anne told me she worked as a journalist, but that must have been before everything went online. Roberta continues to be a mystery woman."

At Good Shepherd, the sight of Eileen pushing Ray's wheelchair into the activities room drew Janet out of her rumination over Roberta and how she would react when the elderly woman walked through the door. Harry came in behind them with Crosby dressed in a new dog sweater. It had writing on the back. THE SNUGGLE IS REAL. When Janet read it, she chuckled, and Eileen and Ray came over to see what was so funny.

Janet rubbed the pup's ears. "Crosby, that sweater just made my day."

The gleam in Harry's eyes told Janet that he'd recovered from Friday's slump. "You like it? It was a Christmas gift from an old railroad buddy of mine."

"I might need to find one for Laddie."

Kate pushed the big whiteboard to the front of the room and turned it around to write something on it.

When Roberta walked in, she came right over and wrapped her arm around Janet's shoulder. "Kate told me you said yes to the celebration dinner," she said in a quiet voice. She gave Janet a grandmotherly squeeze. "It means a lot to both of us."

The kindness in Roberta's tone resurrected the feelings Janet had about her when she left the note for Harry on the corkboard. At that moment, Roberta didn't seem capable of stealing from the same location where she'd expressed encouraging words to a sweet old man.

Janet returned Roberta's embrace and whispered back, "We're excited about it too." She and Debbie already had plans to look through Charla's stash of tablecloths after closing the café for the day.

"Do me a favor." Roberta lowered her voice even more. "When you figure out the cost of the food for the dinner, let me know. I'd like to cover it."

"Are you sure?"

"Absolutely." She patted Janet's shoulder. "Tell Kate an anonymous donor pitched in."

Janet whispered back, "Okay."

Kate clapped her hands. "Good morning, everyone. If you can take your seats, I have another exciting announcement."

A few last-minute stragglers scrambled to remove their coats and claim the closest chairs like middle schoolers fearing being kept after class for being late. Janet took her seat beside Nora and greeted her with a pat on the arm.

The same yellow legal pad sat blank on the table in front of Nora. "I didn't scare you away yet, huh?"

Janet shook her head. "Nope. Sorry to disappoint you."

Kate looked directly at her grandmother and Janet. "Enough socializing, ladies."

Nora nudged Janet. She raised her eyebrows, her eyes gleaming in a way that Janet found refreshing. "See, I'm a bad influence on you."

Janet responded with a playful, "Shush, you're going to get us in trouble."

Kate folded her hands in front of her. "I'm glad to see that the two of you have become such good friends." She walked over to the whiteboard and rested her hand on the side of it. "Actually, I have two fun pieces of news this morning. I'll start with the most exciting. I am so thrilled about our anthology that I want to celebrate the project properly." She turned the board around to reveal the big announcement.

WEDNESDAY, JANUARY 31
BOOK LAUNCH PARTY
6:00 P.M. AT THE WHISTLE STOP CAFÉ

"Before any of you start to worry that you can't make it because of transportation, I'm in the process of taking care of that. Feel free to invite a family member or friend. Just be sure to let me know as soon as possible so I can give Janet and Debbie a head count."

Seeing the excitement on Eileen's face, and even Nora's, made the anticipation of transforming the café into a formal dining room worth every extra errand and hour of planning.

Someone in the back asked, "How much will the dinner cost?"

Kate looked across the room at Janet. A hint of anxiousness clouded her eyes. "There's no charge."

Janet stood. "Debbie and I are excited to have you. Dress up, bring a friend, and prepare for a fun night to reward yourself for your hard work." She sat back down. "I'll even splurge on some bleed-free pens for autographing your books."

Kate smiled. "Or we can pass around your fancy fountain pen."

Janet's stomach clenched. She forced herself to smile back. "Whatever we do, it'll be great."

Kate's second announcement unfolded after she finished a short teaching segment on how to prepare a story for the anthology. Three class members from the community had offered to join Janet, Roberta, and the assistant that Good Shepherd provided in helping the older attendees get their stories written. They volunteered to either transcribe what their classmates shared or type the handwritten stories. It touched Janet to watch seniors from the community sacrifice the writing portion of their workshop time in order to assist the oldest Good Shepherd residents. The days of residents feeling overwhelmed by the writing process were a thing of the past. While Kate worked with Eileen, Janet pulled up a chair across from Nora, hoping she could end the hour with a few words on her legal pad.

"So, are you ready to tell me about the story you came up with?"

Nora looked down at her blank legal pad. For the first time that morning, Janet noticed that it seemed thinner than it was last Wednesday. She saw the ragged evidence of page after page having been torn from the notepad.

"I thought I had, but every time I start writing about my younger days, I get hung up inside. My life hasn't exactly been like one of those feel-good movies on TV."

Janet leaned in and said softly, "You aren't alone, Nora. I bet there are many in this room who can say the same thing." She thought of the little she'd learned about Nora during last Wednesday's class—that she worked as a teacher and that her father died in the war. "This is just an idea, but maybe you can write about being raised by a single mom at a time when they didn't have the resources that women have now."

"That would be a grand idea, except I wasn't raised by a single mom. Not for long anyway."

While Janet searched her mind for a sensitive way to ask who had raised her, Nora started peeling away the shreds at the top of her legal pad. "After Dad's funeral, Mom could hardly get out of bed. She couldn't handle things on her own like she did when he was overseas. If you want to know the truth, she was always easily over-whelmed, but looking back, I think she managed as long as she was getting letters from Daddy and had hope of his return. As soon as she knew he wasn't coming home…" Nora frowned. "She got sick. She passed a month after Daddy." She dropped the paper shreds in a little pile.

"How old were you?"

"Almost seven. My big brother, Steven, was ten."

"I'm so sorry."

Nora went on with her story as if Janet hadn't spoken. "Stevie and I went to live with relatives—me with Mama's sister's family and Stevie with Mama's brother and sister-in-law, who didn't have children of their own."

"You couldn't stay together?"

"Times were hard. It was a lot to take in one child, let alone two."

"That must have been very difficult for you." Janet wanted so badly to say something less trite than that, but nothing came. Part of her was still getting over the shock of Nora opening up to her.

"I got to see my brother every Sunday at church. Then my uncle lost his job and had to cut corners. Me being one of the corners. I went to live with my grandparents in Cincinnati. They saw to it that Stevie and I had a visit at least once a year. We'd all ride the train down here for a week during the summer."

Janet struggled to find a response to Nora being able to see her brother only once a year.

Nora clicked her pen. "They were good to me. Grandma and Grandpa, I mean."

"I'm glad."

Nora suddenly smacked her notepad. "You know what all those hard things taught me? I learned not to rely on other people or expect life to come wrapped up in a pretty bow. I worked hard, went to college, became a teacher, and kept my job even after I was married to a doctor and no longer needed to. So if something happened to my husband, I would have the means to support myself and my children. I vowed to be strong for my kids' sake. Maybe I was too tough on them sometimes, but it kept me from letting tragedy do me in like it did my mother."

Janet let Nora's words sink in. "That doesn't sound depressing to me."

Nora rolled her pen over the top of her notepad. "You're just saying that so I'll write something."

"No, I'm not," Janet said. "I mean, I do want you to write something. I want you to have a story in the anthology, like everyone else. And I also think what you told me would make a powerful story. I don't picture you writing about how tragic your life was. I see you writing about what a strong person you became despite all the loss."

Nora's eyes grew moist. "Maybe I will. Thanks, Janet. You're a good listener. That's a good trait to have."

Nora's compliment came so unexpectedly that Janet had no idea how to respond. She squeezed Nora's hand. "I enjoy listening to you." She scooted her chair back. "How about if I give you some space to write, now that you have an idea, and go see how Harry is doing?"

Nora nodded. "Okay." She held up her white pen with the Good Shepherd logo on it. "I'll let you read it when I'm done."

"I can hardly wait."

On her way to check on Harry, Janet recognized why Nora's comment about being a good listener hit her so deeply. She'd grown used to hearing, "You're the best baker in town," but "You're a good listener"? That she didn't hear very often. *Maybe because baking doesn't require a lot of listening and getting to know new people.*

When she walked over to Harry, he was staring off into the distance, the page in front of him half filled with words. It wasn't until Janet sat down beside him that she realized his eyes were focused on Roberta, who sat a few feet away helping Ray find a focus for a story about his first Christmas as a soldier.

"Need any help, Harry?"

He jumped like being startled out of sleep. "Hey there, Janet." His eyes drifted back to where Roberta and Ray sat.

Janet scooted her chair a little closer to Harry and rested her folded arms on the table. "How about if you talk to her after class? It makes me sad to watch you torment yourself."

Harry picked up his pen again. "No need to worry. I'm not tormenting myself. I'm writing what I wish I could say to that little girl I let down all those years ago."

Instead of leaving as soon as class ended, Janet lingered under the guise of helping with cleanup until everyone left, including Roberta.

As much as she didn't want to ruin the good feeling of helping Nora come up with a story, Janet couldn't shake Kate's comment about using the fountain pen to autograph books during the launch party. She would rather tell Kate now than to have her find out when she saw the pen missing at the café and possibly make a big deal about it in front of customers.

She tossed a handful of empty creamer cups into the trash can. *Please help me word this, God.* "Kate, before I go, I need to tell you something." She walked over as Kate was pushing the whiteboard into a corner. "You mentioned wanting to use the fountain pen during the party."

"I'm sorry. I should have asked. I seem to be jumping ahead of myself constantly these days."

"It's not that. I love the idea of using it for the book-launch party, but…" She braced herself for Kate's reaction. "I no longer have it. It disappeared. Last Wednesday, I went to put it away after Debbie and I closed the café, and it was gone."

Kate sank into a folding chair. "Oh, Janet. I had a feeling this would happen."

"Debbie and I are hoping it will roll out from under a chair or that a customer will come in saying they found it in the waiting area, the restroom, or some other weird place that we haven't torn apart yet." *Was there any such place?* "But for now, it's gone."

Kate shook her head. "It was stolen."

Despite her own thoughts about that possibility, it bugged Janet to hear those words from Kate. "Possibly, but like I said, I'm hoping it will turn up."

Kate slapped her knees, heaved a sigh, and stood back up. "Well, that's too bad. It really is. If I..." Kate's hands flew to her temples. "Oh, Janet. I just remembered something."

"What?"

"Harry."

"What about Harry?"

Kate released her grip on her head and looked up at Janet. "I saw Harry with it when Gran and I went to the café on Wednesday afternoon."

"Yes, he used it to write one of his stories for your workshop."

"But I saw him put it in his pocket," Kate said in a conspiratorial whisper. "After he showed that little girl how to use it."

"I saw him do that too. But then he took it out."

"He did it more than once."

"Are you sure?" Janet frowned. "I told Harry what happened the other day, and he immediately offered to go home and check his pockets just in case. He didn't find it."

"That doesn't mean the pen isn't at his house."

Janet had to fight hard to keep from yelling. "What are you implying?"

"Only that he might have taken it."

Janet looked around to make sure no one had come into the activities room. "Harry would never take something that doesn't belong to him."

"He's an old man, Janet. Maybe he got a bit confused and—"

"Harry is as sharp as a tack." It took every ounce of restraint to hold in her anger. "Kate, I know you're trying to be helpful, but Harry is a dear friend of mine and Debbie's. He is a well-respected member of this community. It is possible that someone who was in the café that day took the pen, but I know for a fact it was not Harry Franklin."

Kate backed up and reached under the lecture podium for her purse. "I'm sorry if I offended you. I just know it isn't unheard of for someone to do something we would never expect of them."

# CHAPTER FIFTEEN

*April 29, 1945*

Harry couldn't take his eyes off Sylvia as she closed the door to her aunt's house. He'd gotten used to seeing her in her mechanic jumpsuit, a choir robe, or an ordinary school dress. But today she wore a blue Sunday-best dress and hat, white bobby socks, and brown loafers. She had a silver charm bracelet around her wrist with a charm shaped like the letter S dangling from it. She smelled like the honeysuckle soap his mother used for special occasions.

"That's a pretty bracelet." Harry bit his lip. What guy comments on a girl's bracelet? *He should've complimented her hair or her dress like his brother Lester instructed during their big first-date talk. Sylvia looked like springtime in her blue dress, with her hair down instead of tied up in a scarf for working.*

She held up her wrist and shook it. "Thank you. My aunt gave it to me as a reward for passing my mechanics training test with one hundred percent. She and Mom went in on it."

"You had to take a test?" Sylvia was a smart girl. Next time he wrote her a note, he would pay even closer attention to his penmanship and grammar.

"Not officially, but my aunt gave me one as part of training me to assist her."

Harry offered Sylvia his arm, just like Lester told him to, and led the way down the front steps. "I enjoyed meeting your mother. She and your aunt are really nice." He'd told them he'd have Sylvia home by supper-time. They'd made Sylvia promise not to take more than her share of the desserts, causing a look of embarrassment in her eyes. But all of that faded into the background of finally being on their way to the picnic without any adults around.

Sylvia held his arm until they reached the side-walk. At first he didn't know what to say to her other than commenting on her dress, in an attempt to make up for not doing it right away. It felt strange to talk while strolling through Sylvia's neighborhood instead of at the depot. But as soon as she got him talking about that morning's sermon and Harry remarked on how much he enjoyed the hymn that the choir sang *during the offertory, being with her felt perfectly natural.*

*Walking to the church required going through downtown Dennison, through streets Harry had traveled hundreds of times. Today, those familiar streets looked golden with Sylvia at his side, asking him about classes and his plans after high school.*

*"I hope to keep working for the railroad," Harry told her. "My goal is to be a conductor."*

*"I can see you as a conductor."*

*Harry was getting ready to ask Sylvia about her plans when the sight of a familiar form in front of Carl's Five & Dime almost stopped his heart. It was the man in the red cap, standing beside the entrance, counting some coins in his hand. Seeing the man brought back the image of him swiping a sandwich, the sight of him devouring it, and the promise he'd made to Miss Eileen only to break it.*

*He didn't realize how long he'd gone without talking until Sylvia asked, "You got something on your mind, Harry?"*

*He brushed off the cloud of worry that had started to follow him as soon as he saw the man in the red cap. He didn't want to spoil the afternoon by burdening Sylvia with his worries. "Oh, it's nothing."*

"Are you sure? You got quiet all of a sudden. It might help to talk about it."

Harry felt so touched by Sylvia's thoughtfulness that "Okay, since you asked," flew out before he could stop the words. "Did you see that man in front of Carl's store?"

Sylvia looked over her shoulder. "Yes. I've seen him around town before. My mother thinks he might be off his head, maybe because of the war."

"He hangs around the train station sometimes. Miss Eileen told me to let her know if I saw him again. Some passengers complained about him panhandling."

"I don't think you need to tell her about seeing him now. He's at the Five & Dime, not the train station."

Harry stuffed his hands into the pockets of his trousers. "I'm feeling guilty because I saw him steal a sandwich from the canteen table while the volunteers were setting up. I didn't tell Miss Eileen or anyone at the canteen." Why was he telling Sylvia so much? This was a date.

"You should have said something if he stole." Her eyes bored into him, but in a way that reminded him to do the right thing, not in a way that left him feeling ashamed of himself.

"I know I should have. But he looks so poor. What if he has a family to take care of?"

"That's really nice of you, Harry. But him being down on his luck doesn't make it okay to hang out pan-handling and swiping sandwiches that are meant for the soldiers."

Harry saw the church in the distance. "I know."

"And if he has a family, it won't help them if he ends up in jail for stealing. Next time he might be tempted to take more than a sandwich."

"That's a good point." Maybe having someone as good-hearted as Miss Eileen reprimand him after he took the sandwich would've made that man think twice about doing such a thing again. And who knew? She might have given him something to help his family. "Thanks for listening, Sylvia."

"Anytime."

As they approached the church, Harry put the man in the red cap out of his mind.

Sylvia stopped in front of the gravel path leading to the sanctuary, where they'd been told to meet to pray for the troops before the picnic. "You know what, Harry? It's nice of you to care about that man. Most people would just turn him in without a thought for what he might be going through. We need more people like you in the world."

Her words were so sweet, Harry felt the lingering shadow of seeing that man drift away. "You're a pretty nice person yourself." He offered his arm again. "Are you hungry?"

"Starved. I hope they have chocolate pie. That's my favorite."

Harry noted that for the next time he asked Sylvia on a date.

# CHAPTER SIXTEEN

anet slammed the flat side of the fork into the peanut butter cookie dough ball. She continued creating crisscrosses on the row of balls with much more force than necessary. She usually baked in the morning at the café, not in the afternoon, but keeping her hands busy with ingredients and baking utensils was the only thing preventing her from stomping around the kitchen and muttering unkind things about Kate under her breath. The activity finally allowed her body to relax at the sound of Debbie flipping the sign in the window to Closed.

Debbie joined her in the kitchen just as Janet shoved the tray in the oven and grabbed a spatula for a tray of cookies that had come out moments ago. She would take them home to Ian if Debbie thought they wouldn't be fresh enough for customers tomorrow.

Debbie reached out and took the spatula from Janet. She set it on the counter. "What's up, my friend? You've been upset ever since you came back from Good Shepherd."

Her friend's sensitivity caused Janet to pause from taking her aggressions out on cookie dough and almost triggered tears. She fought to keep her voice steady so she could explain without having a full-on meltdown and turned to face the friend who had shared so many emotional moments with her over the years. "We have to find that fountain pen."

"We tried. We practically tore the dining room apart last week."

"Are you sure we looked everywhere?"

"Everywhere including along the train tracks." Debbie touched Janet's arm. "Hey. What's going on?"

"I told Kate about the pen."

"Did she react that badly? It's not like you to be intimidated by someone like her."

Janet took the spatula back from Debbie. "She accused Harry of taking it." Just thinking about it made her hurt for Harry. She lifted two cookies off the sheet. "After this morning's class, I told her the pen was missing because she mentioned having it available for people to autograph their books with during the celebration dinner." She let the cookies fall onto the cooling rack. "It was shocking how quickly she jumped from her anticipated 'I knew it' reaction to 'I think Harry Franklin did it.' She said she saw him put it in his pocket the day it went missing."

"I saw him put it in his pocket a couple times too. But both times he took it out. He was writing the story about when he got it. So, naturally, I assumed he was reliving that moment. Which would make perfect sense to anyone who knows him."

"But Kate doesn't know him, so she jumped to the worst possible scenario. Oh, and she even had the gall to suggest that he took it because he's an old man and got confused." Janet dropped the spatula onto the counter with a clank. "I'm sorry to get so worked up over this. It just upsets me to have someone accuse a friend of doing something he wouldn't do in a million years. If Harry knew Kate thought he stole from us, it would break his heart. He's one of the most dedicated members of her workshop." She grabbed the spatula again and poured her frustration into freeing cookies from the baking sheet.

Debbie took a cookie off the cooling rack. "Knowing what I do about Kate, she probably thought she was being helpful. It still makes me mad that she pointed the finger at Harry though." She took a big bite of her cookie then went to the refrigerator and came back with a jug of milk. "If not for him and the rest of the seniors in that workshop, I would want to pull out of the dinner right now."

"I feel the same way." Janet took two glasses from the drying rack and grabbed a cookie for herself. "As angry as I am on Harry's behalf, I don't want to disappoint our friends by canceling because of Kate." She broke her cookie in half.

Debbie poured milk into both glasses and pushed one toward Janet. "We'll give that class the best dinner imaginable, and you'll help them write the best stories they can."

"In the meantime, we need to figure out what happened to the fountain pen before Kate starts a rumor that Harry took it."

Janet poked at the plate of spaghetti in front of her while Ian twirled the noodles around his fork. "I just don't understand people, Ian. Even after I told her Harry already checked his pockets, she still wouldn't let it go."

Ian lifted a forkful of noodles. "Well, she doesn't know and love Harry like you do."

"Debbie said Kate doesn't seem like herself right now." Janet moved her fork from her spaghetti to her salad. After drowning her sorrows in peanut butter cookies with Debbie instead of looking through their mothers' party supplies, her stomach screamed for something to offset the sweetness. "Maybe Kate took the fountain pen." She stabbed a bunch of greens. "Sorry. I'm just mad."

Ian set his fork down. "People have been known to accuse others of a crime they committed themselves. Would Kate have a reason to want to steal something like a valuable pen?"

"I don't know her well enough to answer that."

"Do you think it's possible she took the pen for her brother-in-law?"

Janet replayed her interactions with Kate the day the pen disappeared, how long she was in the café, and any opportunities she might have had to take something. "I guess it's possible. But why blame Harry?"

"It might help to find out a little more about her."

Janet rubbed her forehead. "Maybe I'm overthinking this because I'm tired and feeling protective of Harry.

Ian patted her arm. "Try not to think about it anymore tonight. Get some sleep, pray about it, and start fresh tomorrow. God has ways of bringing things to light when we stop trying so hard."

"You're right." But why did it feel so significant that the first person to point out the pen's value was also the first person to point fingers?

An hour before her alarm was due to go off, Janet woke up to Laddie's high-pitched "I need to go outside" bark.

"Really? Right now?" she moaned into her pillow. "But it's so dark and cold."

Laddie's bark and frantic pacing by the bedroom door confirmed he couldn't wait.

Ian rolled over. "Do you want me to take this shift?" His question brought back memories of the month when infant Tiffany decided sleeping was for wimps.

"No." Janet sat up. "I have to get up soon anyway." She put on her robe, picked up her phone, turned off her alarm, and met Laddie at the bedroom door. "Come on, little man."

Janet shivered while waiting for Laddie, thankful that the cold would keep him from turning the pit stop into playtime. He ran back in and over to his dog bed. Janet yawned and started a pot of coffee. She read a devotional on her Bible app and sent up a fervent prayer for God to send her a post-New Year's miracle and help her find the fountain pen for Harry's sake. She got up to fill a mug with coffee and took a sip. *Thank You, Lord, for creating coffee beans.* She smiled. *A good cup of coffee is just one more way You show Your love for us.*

The earlier-than-usual quiet made her drowsy even after several sips of coffee. She picked up her phone again and gave in to the pull to engage in some mindless scrolling. Ian's point about how helpful it would be to know more about Kate came back to her. She entered *Katherine Lipton Cleveland, OH* into the search bar and asked herself what exactly it was she expected to find. An arrest record for stealing fine writing instruments or a history of pilfering items and pinning the blame on innocent old men? Still, she waited for the results. If nothing else, she would understand what kind of person she was dealing with.

At first, all she found were the usual directory listings, the website for the glass company Debbie told her about, and links to a social media account set to Private. Within thirty seconds, she'd hit *Request to Follow* and started feeling like a stalker. She clicked on a link to *Lipton Windows & Glass*. Doug and Kate Lipton were pictured as the photo-perfect owners.

Janet puckered her lips and blew out slowly. None of this added up to anything.

Then a note at the top of the Welcome page caught her eye. *Lipton Windows & Glass has permanently closed its doors. Thank you for your business.*

Janet stopped. Debbie had never said anything about Kate's business closing. It had to have happened recently.

She hit the back arrow and spotted another result that she'd missed before. LOCAL BUSINESS OWNERS FACE LAWSUIT. The blurb underneath the headline included Lipton Windows & Glass. Janet hovered her finger over the article link. *Maybe this is none of my business.*

Then she thought of Harry and Kate's accusation.

*I need to understand why Kate would blame Harry. Besides, it's a public article.*

She tapped on the link.

# CHAPTER SEVENTEEN

When Debbie walked through the doors of the café, Janet was putting two gingerbread loaves into the oven. Part of her regretted reading the article she'd found. If such a thing were part of her recent history and, worse yet, public knowledge, it would be humiliating to know just anyone could find the information on the internet.

Debbie dropped her purse behind the counter. "Hey, you. Are you feeling better this morning?"

Janet shut the oven. "Much better. I had a good talk with Ian last night and slept like a rock." She set the timer and started gathering ingredients for maple scones. "Then I got up to let the dog out, did my morning devotions, and googled Kate Lipton in order to prove she blamed Harry for stealing the fountain pen because she's a terrible person. So basically, I started my day with doing exactly the opposite of what I imagine God would want me to do after time in His Word." She reached for a large bowl. "Now in addition to being mad at Kate, I feel sorry for her."

Janet waited for Debbie to ask why.

Debbie opened the pantry. "Join the club. Last night an old friend from my church in Cleveland called, and I caught myself finding creative ways to bring Kate into the conversation. Now that

I know more, I understand why she hasn't been acting like herself lately."

Janet plunged a measuring cup into a tub of flour. "So you know Kate and her husband got sued after an improper glass installation that injured five people?"

"Yep. I don't know if the article you read mentioned this, but Doug and Kate ended up settling to avoid going to court. Even with that, in addition to having to close their business, they ended up with a ton of debt and are now in the process of losing their home and going through a divorce. Apparently, the accident happened two weeks after I moved to Dennison."

Janet added baking powder and salt. "I feel even worse now. It sounds like they'd already had some complaints about faulty installations before the accident."

Debbie released a sigh. "It was a mess. According to this friend, the accident happened at a deli owned by relatives of a family that Doug and Kate knew really well. As you can imagine, the friendship dissolved instantly, but other friends turned their backs because of what happened, including church friends."

Janet poured in some sugar. "That explains why Kate came here planning to stay for an entire month by herself."

Debbie came out of the pantry with a bag of coffee. "If her financial situation is as bad as it sounds, I'm surprised she was so eager to buy baked goods from the café and pay extra for delivery."

Janet went to the refrigerator for butter. "I didn't even think about that. And the celebration dinner. Roberta offered to pay for the food, but Kate doesn't know that yet. How did she plan to pay for it?"

"Good question. Maybe she's still in denial. Between all this and trying to get her grandmother adjusted at Good Shepherd, I don't know how she's holding it together."

"Me neither." Janet sliced the butter into chunks and slid them into the flour mixture. "It still doesn't excuse her accusing Harry of stealing the pen."

"No, it doesn't."

Janet's breath caught. Kate had debt. Lots of debt. She had access to something her brother-in-law wanted.

*It doesn't excuse her blaming Harry, but it might explain it.*

---

Janet set Patricia's peppermint mocha in front of her and handed her a fork for her gingerbread. "So, Patricia. I have a legal question."

Patricia took a sip of her mocha. "Sure. What do you want to know?"

"Let's say a business owner gets sued but settles out of court. Can they lose their home in the process?"

Patricia twirled a spoon in her mug. "It's possible. Settling out of court can still involve paying a lot of money. They just avoid the court fees and a long legal process. Business owners usually have liability insurance, but it doesn't necessarily cover everything, and if they already have a lot of debt and can't keep up with their mortgage payments, then yes, their house could end up in foreclosure."

Once again, Janet thought back to the day when Kate saw the fountain pen for the first time. Her protective reaction to something that wasn't even hers was almost comical. Definitely uncalled for.

"Now, let's say the lawsuit involved multiple injuries. What sort of settlement would they most likely pay?"

Patricia puffed her cheeks and blew out slowly. "It depends on the injuries and a lot of other factors. But let me put it this way. Quite a bit."

"So basically, they would be digging themselves out of the hole for a long time."

Patricia nodded. "Without great liability insurance, yes."

"I bet it's not uncommon for something like this to affect a couple's marriage."

"Not at all uncommon." She wrapped her hands around her mug and started to take a sip then stopped. "Wait. Is everything okay? You and Debbie aren't—"

"No. We're fine. Ian and I are fine too. Sorry to be so cryptic. I'm just looking into something." Janet set an extra napkin beside Patricia's plate. "It's part of the ongoing fountain pen saga. The longer it's missing, the more I'm leaning toward thinking it was stolen. My mind is running wild with theories about who might have taken it. Anyway, thanks."

"I don't blame you a bit for considering it stolen and trying to figure out who took it. But what does a hypothetical lawsuit have to do with a missing fountain pen?"

"It's hard to explain without possibly sharing more than I should." Janet rested her hands on the counter, mentally fatigued from playing detective with nothing to go on but unsettling conversations. "Have you ever known anyone who got into a situation like the one I just put out there?"

"Unfortunately, yes."

"I imagine being sued would really mess with a person emotionally. Even if they were at fault."

"Oh, for sure. It's humiliating. And if the person was at fault, they might carry around a lot of shame, along with the reality that their days of owning a business are most likely over. The burden of debt is a constant reminder."

Janet's suspicions were suddenly mixed with unexpected compassion for Kate. "All the debt could make a person pretty desperate, I bet."

Patricia took another sip of her coffee. "Sometimes. Then there are those who learn from their mistakes, try not to let what happened define them, and rebuild their lives." She set her mug down. "Okay, now I'm intrigued."

"Trust me, as soon as I feel comfortable sharing, I'll fill you in."

"If I can help in any way, let me know."

"I definitely will."

"It's really a shame that the pen hasn't turned up. I even caught myself looking in *my* pockets and purse. And I wasn't even in the café the afternoon it disappeared."

"I've been doing the same thing. I've checked every apron and tote bag that had contact with the café last week. I checked under every bench in the depot and on the platform outside. Debbie and I even walked along the train tracks in case someone felt guilty and dumped it after they got out of the café." Janet looked around to make sure Harry hadn't come in. She lowered her voice to be safe. "I was going to give it to your grandpa after taking the message board down at the end of the month. He used it to write one of his stories. He says he once had a fountain pen just like it but gave it away."

"Oh yeah, he mentioned that to me too. He told me the story of when he got it. I can picture him as a teenager, picking up that man's wallet off the ground and running as fast as he could to return it to the owner. I can also see him recognizing someone else's need to have the pen and giving it away without thinking twice about it."

"That's one of the reasons I wanted to give it to him. That, and because I have a sneaking suspicion that the one I bought used to be his."

"Wouldn't that be something?"

"Only if we find it. If not, the idea of having your grandpa's pen and losing it so quickly would just be sad."

# CHAPTER EIGHTEEN

The next morning, Janet arrived at Good Shepherd with a plate of gingerbread and a surprise in her pocket for the one attendee she knew didn't care for it. She purposely avoided pre-workshop interactions with Kate by going to the kitchen to fill two pitchers of water while attendees trickled in chatting about their stories and how shockingly difficult it was to get words from their heads to the page.

She passed Roberta on her way back to the activities room.

Roberta reached for one of the pitchers. "Let me take one of those off your hands."

Janet took her up on the offer, relieved to have both a free hand and an unexpected opportunity for a one-on-one with the mysterious woman. "Hey, Roberta, I'm curious. If you live in San Francisco, how do you know Kate?"

"We met at a writing conference in New Mexico, of all places. We kept in touch, became good friends, and now here we are." She said hello to a resident they passed in the hallway. "I confess that I've been having so much fun helping her with this class that I've neglected to reach out to family members I have in the area. But Kate needs me right now."

Janet ached to hear more about that from Roberta's perspective. "Are you enjoying your stay?"

"Oh yes. It's nice to be home. We moved out of Dennison before I turned eleven, but being here and spending time at the café where I can remember days of hanging around the station brings back so many memories."

Janet stopped outside the activities room. "If you used to hang around the station, you must have known Harry Franklin then." Putting it that way seemed a lot more diplomatic than "I've noticed how you look at him and how uncomfortable he is in your presence."

"I knew him very well." She chuckled. "I'm not sure he recognizes me after so many years. Not that it surprises me. I believe the word *scrappy* would describe me back then. That, and way too curious for my own good."

Janet took hold of the door handle. "I know for a fact he recognizes you."

Roberta stopped at the doorway. She held the door open for Janet and glanced in the direction of where Harry sat with Ray and Eileen. "Is that so? It's good to know. We have some catching up to do then."

During the short break between Kate's teaching and the students' writing time, Janet watched Nora push her walker over to the refreshments table. Janet reached into her tote bag and pulled out a big chocolate chip cookie wrapped in cellophane. When she walked up beside Nora, she noticed that her eyes seemed glued to the plate of gingerbread.

Janet put the cookie behind her back.

Nora took a paper cup. "Gingerbread Lady strikes again." A much different tone came through in her greeting.

*Is she fighting tears?* Janet tried to get a closer look at Nora's face without making it too obvious. Sure enough, her eyes were glistening.

"Yeah. Sorry about that. Some of the others requested it the other day."

"Majority rule, I suppose." She continued to gaze at the gingerbread. "It's just as well. I'm watching my figure anyway." She smirked.

"Oh, I didn't forget about you." Janet whipped the cookie out from behind her back. "Ta-da! Surprise."

Nora's smirk spread into a full smile. "Aw. That is sweet of you. Literally." She took the cookie. "Thank you."

Janet squeezed Nora's thin shoulder. "I can't have someone go without treats."

Nora set her cup in front of Janet. "And to think I was considering trying a slice of your gingerbread just to see what all the fuss is about."

"You don't have to."

Nora slipped the cookie into her pocket and reached for a plate. "No. I want to." Her hand trembled. "I haven't had it since I was a little girl. Mama used to make it."

Janet chose the nicest-looking slice on the plate, slid a fork under it, and moved it to Nora's plate. "I hope this is as good as your mama's."

"We'll see."

"Go sit at your table. I'll bring this and your drink to you."

Nora gave her pocket a protective pat. "I'm still holding on to the cookie."

"Of course. If you decide the gingerbread was a mistake, you'll have that as a backup."

Nora scooted herself to her table. "Or a snack for later."

"Exactly." Janet set down Nora's plate. "What would you like in your coffee?"

"Two sugars and two half-and-halfs, please, madame."

"Coming right up."

While preparing Nora's coffee, Janet saw Roberta stop at Harry's table to chat. Roberta gave Crosby a pat then sat beside Eileen. Janet barely had time to fully revel in that moment before Kate took Roberta's place at Harry's side. Janet took the long way to deliver Nora's coffee in hopes of catching what Kate had to say to him. She passed Harry's table as Kate said, "If you could take another quick look, I would appreciate it so much."

"I'd be happy to," Harry said. He opened his notebook and went back to writing.

Everything in Janet wanted to give Kate some serious stink eye when they passed each other behind Nora's chair. *Take the high road,* Janet commanded herself.

"Coffee is served." Janet set Nora's cup on the table and sat down beside her.

Nora sniffed, still chewing a bite of gingerbread. When she swallowed it, she closed her eyes tightly. She set her fork down and brushed a tear away. "Thanks."

Janet reached out and took Nora's hand. Nora linked her fingers through Janet's and cleared her throat. "That's *some* gingerbread."

"Can I get you anything else? Or maybe we can take a walk and talk."

Nora let go of Janet's hand and took another bite. She chewed it slowly. "No. If you don't mind, I think I'd like to go back to my room." She took a sip of coffee, pushed her plate away, and reached for her walker. "I have a laptop in there." She picked up her legal pad. "I know what I want to write about now. But I think I need to be alone to do it."

❧

When class ended, Janet wanted to find Nora's room and check on her before returning to the café. But something deep in her heart urged her to give Nora privacy to write her story. Besides, Kate would most likely go straight there, and after overhearing her questioning Harry, Kate was the last person Janet wanted to deal with.

Harry was too engrossed in a conversation with Ray for Janet to ask him about his writing progress, so she picked up her plate and prepared to return to her café comfort zone. She and Debbie planned to sit down and hash out the menu for the celebration dinner as soon as the café closed for the day, and every extra moment in Kate's presence robbed her of a smidgen of joy over creating a meaningful event for the class.

She brushed crumbs off the plate into the trash can and called goodbye to Kate, who waved in response. She was occupied with reading something on her phone. Janet took her gloves out of her jacket pocket and watched Harry, his head down, walk out of the activities room with Ray.

That did it. Janet swung her tote bag over her shoulder, gripped her plate to her chest, and strutted in Kate's direction. "Kate, I need to say something."

Kate set her phone aside. Distress fogged her eyes. "Sure. What's up?" Her voice lacked the bravado from Monday, or even her charisma during today's class.

Janet's heart stirred as she pulled up a chair to sit across from Kate. She looked into Kate's eyes and detected a weariness. Would confronting her right this minute really help Harry? "It was nice to hear your grandmother say she came up with a story."

"Is that why she left class?"

"Yes. She needed some space, I think."

"Roberta is checking on her now."

Janet's anger faded at the sight of Kate rubbing the bridge of her nose like she was fighting off a headache. "Hey, are you okay?"

"I'm fine. Just exhausted." She picked up her phone.

"It must be overwhelming, getting your grandmother adjusted all by yourself. Are you her only family?"

Kate let her hands drop in her lap. "No, her youngest son—my dad's brother—lives ten minutes from here. My parents are close by as well."

Yet Kate drove all the way from Cleveland to take charge while in the process of losing her home and her marriage?

"Do they help at all?"

Kate rested one hand on her small waist and ran her other hand through her hair. "Um. No. Not really. They stopped by over the weekend for a visit, but I'm pretty much in charge of the rest."

"That must be so stressful with…" Janet stopped herself before spilling facts that Kate didn't know she had. "Leading the workshop and trying to sell her house."

"It is, but Gran is worth it. I know she can be a pill. But a lot of that attitude is an act. She hasn't had an easy life. Throw in her husband passing away last year and surgery not making the difference she was hoping for. Thanks for being so patient with her."

"I'm happy to do it. I get a kick out of her."

"That's one way to put it."

Roberta walked in as Janet got up to leave. Kate stuck her phone in her pocket.

"Your gran is doing just fine. She's typing away," Roberta said to Kate.

"What a relief." Kate held her arm out to Roberta. "I wouldn't have survived the past year without this lady over here." She wrapped her arm around Roberta's waist and leaned against her. "We're having an extended slumber party at Gran's house this month, since I twisted her arm to help me with this workshop."

Roberta gave Kate a squeeze. "Not that it took much twisting. I'm having the time of my life working with everyone in the class and connecting with old friends." She looked down at Kate. "Besides, I'd do anything for dear Kate. I never had children of my own, so God sent me her."

Seeing the warm connection between the two women, Janet thanked God that she hadn't confronted Kate. Roberta would have walked in on that tense moment. "I better get back to the café."

She turned to go. At the door to the activities room, she spotted the plastic wrap from her plate and stooped down to grab it.

"He just called me." Kate spoke softly.

The sound of a chair scraping across the floor almost caused Janet to turn around. She forced her body to stay put, facing the doorway.

Roberta asked, "How much?"

Janet crumpled the plastic and dropped it in the trash can. She strained to hear more. All she caught was Roberta trying to comfort Kate. "It's going to be okay. I promise."

# CHAPTER NINETEEN

*Y*ou didn't confront her?" Debbie sounded more confused than upset. "After what you overheard her say to Harry?"

Janet tidied the note cards on the writing desk. "I was ready to. Then I saw Kate's face and knew it wasn't the right time." She pushed an extra tack into a card that was in danger of falling off the message board. Someone had written BE BRAVE TODAY in bright red letters. *Lord, was I really right to wait, or did I miss out on a chance to be brave for Harry's sake?* She considered something that came to her on the drive back to the café. "If she is convinced that Harry took the pen, trying to persuade her otherwise with no evidence to go on except the same points I made last time won't do any good."

"True. What you need is evidence that someone else took it."

Janet was about to tell Debbie what she overheard in the activities room when Debbie said, "Enough about Kate."

"Yes. And enough about the fountain pen for now. Like my grandma used to say whenever she saw me frantically searching for something I lost, 'you'll probably find it when you aren't looking for it.'"

Debbie retrieved her laptop from her tote bag and sat at a table in the back corner of the café. "Are you ready to plan the best dinner of our careers as café owners?"

"I sure am." She flipped the Open sign to Closed, removed her apron, and took a seat across from Debbie.

Debbie opened her laptop. "First, some good news. Not only did Greg agree to be our maître d', but he has a tux from his best friend's wedding. It's decades old, but it still fits, and he agreed to wear it for our event."

"I can't wait to see Greg in a tux." Or to see the expression on Debbie's face when she saw Greg in a tux. "Ian is on board too, and Paulette is looking forward to helping. What about Charla and Greg's boys?"

"Charla is thrilled about helping you in the kitchen, and Jaxon and Julian are excited about being our waiters. Especially when I mentioned they'd probably clean up in tips."

Janet heard a knock on the café door. "Now all we need is a great meal for our guests." She got up to see who was there. "Are we expecting a delivery this afternoon?"

"No," Debbie said. "It's probably Kim. She mentioned stopping by with a pile of records this afternoon."

Instead of seeing Kim at the door, Janet found Harry standing there.

"Hey, Harry. We just closed. Can I get you something to go?"

Harry twisted Crosby's leash around his hand. "Do you have a few minutes?"

Janet swung the door wide. "Sure. Come on in. Debbie and I are planning the dinner for the book launch party, so if you have any requests, now's the time to sneak one in." She pulled out a chair for him. "Have a seat."

"I don't want to keep you." Harry sat in the chair that Janet offered. "So I'll make it quick."

Janet sat back down across from him, and Harry encouraged Crosby to settle at his feet. "I guess it's best to just come out and say it. I know Kate thinks I took the fountain pen."

Janet opened her mouth, but nothing came out. She glanced at Debbie, who also looked at a loss for words.

"No need to protect my feelings. Yesterday I emailed Kate my fountain pen story to see what she thought of it. This morning she remarked on how much she liked it, but then she started asking me about your lost pen."

Janet sighed. "I know. I overheard her asking you to look for it again."

"Do you ladies think I took it?"

"No way," Janet and Debbie said almost in unison.

"I admit, I did put it in my pocket for a minute. But I didn't have any intention of taking it. I was writing my story and wanted to describe how it felt when that doctor gave it to me. I applied what Kate taught us about incorporating all the senses."

Janet smiled. "Harry, you're the best. If you were taking this writing class for a grade, you would get an A-plus."

"And for the record…" Debbie scooted a little closer to Harry. "I saw you take the pen out of your pocket and continue writing. So did Janet. Enough said."

Harry's whole body relaxed. "That's what I hoped you'd say. I needed to be sure. It upsets me that Kate suspects me. I tore my house apart looking for the pen one more time this afternoon just so I could tell her what I already knew. It isn't there."

"You've done all you can do." Janet got up to pour Harry a cup of coffee to take home with him.

"Kate doesn't know you like Janet and I do," Debbie said. "Based on what I remember about Kate, the next thing you'll get from her is a tearful apology after she feels convicted at two in the morning."

Crosby sat up on his haunches, looking at his master.

Janet put her hand on Crosby's head. "See, even your dog agrees with us."

Harry drew Crosby closer to his side. "I did take something that didn't belong to me once. When I was nine years old, I took a roll of hard candies from Carl's Five & Dime. I did it on a dare. But I felt so guilty afterward that I hid the candy in my sock drawer and never ate a single piece of it. I finally confessed to my parents one night at bedtime after hearing a fiery sermon on the radio. My dad marched me down to the Five & Dime before school the next morning and made me return the candy and tell Mr. Carl what I had done."

Janet almost told him the story about her mom's necklace but didn't want to be one of those friends who cut off someone else's story with her story. "We've all done things we're ashamed of."

"That's right," Debbie said. "Just because you took something when you were nine doesn't make you a thief at ninety-five."

"I know, but I still feel ashamed of what I did. I couldn't bring myself to go into that store again until years later when it changed hands and became a hardware store." He rubbed Crosby's ears. "I still think about what I did every time I go there."

Janet could relate. It had taken four years for her to be able to ask to borrow something from her mom after the locket incident. "I bet you aren't too fond of those rolls of hard candies either."

"No, I'm not," Harry said emphatically. "I guess my dad was right when we had our little talk that night. After we left the Five &

Dime, he made me go to school as usual and wait until he came home from work to discuss the matter. It was the longest day of my life. As soon as he came home, he told me to go to my room. I remember sitting there on my bed, smelling dinner cooking, waiting for him to come in and tan my hide like I deserved. Instead, he sat beside me on the bed and said, 'Harry, I ought to punish you, but I'm not going to this time. I think the burden of knowing you did wrong and the feeling of what happened in that store this morning is worse than anything I could dish out.'" Harry wiped his eye. "I started crying like a baby. Dad gave me a big bear hug and then said, 'But if I ever hear of you taking what isn't yours again, we'll be having a very different conversation.'"

Janet's parents hadn't been quite as merciful. She'd been grounded for two weeks and had to buy a new gold chain for Mom's locket. Goodbye, babysitting money. "Maybe that would be a good story for Kate to read. She would know you don't have it in you to repeat the same mistake."

"For now, I'm almost finished with the one I told you about." He glanced at Debbie. "You're welcome to read it too. I promised Patricia a copy."

Debbie playfully slapped the table. "I can hardly wait to read it. You're finding a new talent, Harry."

He stood up. "I don't know how talented I am when it comes to this writing gig, but it feels good to share my stories. And to get a few things off my chest in the process."

# CHAPTER TWENTY

*April 30, 1945*

*Harry watched the five o'clock eastbound train pull away. He pushed the empty baggage cart across the platform past the bench just outside the depot. His mind swirled with so many memories from attending the youth picnic with Sylvia that he had to force himself to concentrate on his work. He saw Birdie on a bench outside the waiting area.*

*"You should go home, Birdie. It'll be getting dark soon. I'm sure your mother wants you home in time for supper."*

*Birdie continued scribbling away with what looked like a new pencil. Her camera hung around her neck and under her arm. Her messenger cap had slipped to one side. "I just need to finish this paragraph."*

*"Sylvia is about to go home and said she'll walk with you to the corner of your street. She's inside*

talking to Miss Eileen." Sylvia's aunt had given her the responsibility of sharing the good news that a second freight car was fully repaired and ready to go.

Birdie pulled an eraser out of her blazer pocket. "Okay."

It was unusual to see Birdie at the station alone, especially on a Monday evening. She and her sister usually came on Saturdays. "Where's Margaret today?"

Birdie looked up from her composition book. "With her friends. She saw some of them when we were going to the market for Mama after school. They started talking about a dance they're going to at school on Friday night. I told her we needed to get going, but she told me to scram, so I came here."

"Your mom's probably wondering what happened to her groceries."

"Maggie said she'd take care of it."

Harry opened the door to the depot and pushed the luggage cart through. "I have some things to do inside, but Sylvia will be out soon. You be ready, okay?"

"I will." She set her composition book, pencil, and eraser aside, picked up her camera, and held it in front of her eyes. "Hey, Harry."

Harry had one hand on the door and the other on the end of the luggage cart. "Yeah?"

"Say cheese."

Before he had a chance to tell Birdie he didn't have time for pictures, Birdie snapped his photo.

"Aw, Birdie. That wasn't nice." He shoved the cart the rest of the way inside. "Just finish your paragraph." He tried not to think about what his face looked like when Birdie snapped the picture. "And stop taking pictures of people without asking. They don't like it."

Birdie snickered and went back to her writing.

While reaching for the doorknob, Harry spotted someone sitting on the far end of the platform. The red cap gave his identity away. He was leaning against the wall, one leg bent and the other hanging off the edge of the platform. He had a cup of something steamy and was eating a sandwich.

Harry saw a few canteen volunteers replenishing their trays. Had that man stolen from the canteen again? Or had one of the volunteers offered him something? Harry couldn't imagine someone being bold enough to eat a stolen sandwich out in the open. Either way, he needed to tell Miss Eileen.

Harry shut the door and parked the luggage cart. He stopped to check the status of the next passenger train and picked up a newspaper left on one of the benches. As he set the newspaper aside for the canteen, he thought of Birdie sitting on the bench and that strange man at the end of the platform. *I should've* had her wait inside. *He could hear Miss Eileen saying goodbye to Sylvia. He was about to go out and fetch Birdie when he heard shouting and a scream from outside. He turned on his heels. "Birdie!"*

*Harry threw open the door leading to the platform. "Miss Eileen," he shouted, "can you help me, please?"*

*Harry found Birdie halfway across the platform, yelling and punching the red-capped man's arm while he yanked at her camera.*

*"Hey," Harry hollered. "Let go of her!"*

*Sylvia and Miss Eileen came running out of the depot, along with Mitch, the other porter on duty. The man let go of Birdie and took off so suddenly that she fell hard onto the platform and against one of the lamp posts. Harry ran to her aid while Mitch took off after the man in the cap.*

*Miss Eileen shouted, "Mitch, don't chase him. We don't need you getting hurt too. I'll call the police."*

*Mitch stopped in his tracks and ran back to the platform. "I'll go with you. I saw which way he ran and what he looked like."*

*Harry wrapped his arm around Birdie's trembling shoulders. "Are you okay?"*

*Sylvia ran over as Harry was helping Birdie up.*

Birdie nodded. "I'm okay." She touched the top of her head. "My cap."

Sylvia found it beside the lamp post and brushed it off. "Here you go, honey." She gently placed it on Birdie's head. "Let's get you inside."

Harry saw a bruise forming on Birdie's forehead and splintery scrapes on both of her knees.

Birdie rubbed her forehead. "He tried to take my camera."

"I know," Harry said. "Miss Eileen is taking care of it right now."

Sylvia took Birdie's hand and led the way to the door. "Let's go inside and get you cleaned up."

Harry kept his arm around Birdie until they were inside and had Birdie settled on the front bench.

Sylvia sat on the other side of Birdie. "What hurts?"

Tears started welling up in Birdie's eyes, but Harry watched her push them back. "Just my knees and my head." She held out her hands. Her palms looked raw from hitting the wood of the platform so hard. "My hands are kind of messed up too."

Sylvia checked them over then stroked her arm. "It's okay now. We'll get you fixed up. Do your folks have a phone?"

"No."

"One of us will go get your mother."

Birdie held up her camera. "I promised Dad I would be careful with this. Now he won't let me use it anymore."

Sylvia reached for the camera. "Let me see it." She brushed the dirt off and examined every inch of it. "It's a little scratched, but the lens looks okay." She handed it back to Birdie. "Your dad will understand that you weren't being careless."

"My notebook. That man grabbed it from me and threw it."

Sylvia hopped up. "I'll go find it."

Harry put his hand on Birdie's shoulder. "Can you wait here for a minute while I find the first-aid kit?"

Birdie checked the elbows of her blazer and brushed them off. "Yes."

At the sight of Birdie rubbing her knees, Harry wished he could relive the afternoon when that man stole a sandwich. He would do things differently. He would go right in and tell Miss Eileen what he saw.

"I'll be right back."

When Harry opened the supply closet, he could hear Miss Eileen on the phone.

"Roberta appears to be okay. But if one of our porters hadn't heard her..."

*Harry's heart sank.* If that porter had done the right thing in the first place, she wouldn't have gotten hurt at all.

*He saw Mitch standing in the doorway of Miss Eileen's office.*

*"Mitch, after you finish, could you go to Birdie's house and tell her mother what happened, so she can come pick her up?"*

*"Sure, Harry. I know right where she lives. Her house is two doors down from mine."*

*After finding the first-aid kit, Harry searched his pocket for his handkerchief and went to the drinking fountain to run cold water over it. When he returned to Birdie's side, Sylvia was coming back in with her composition book and pencil. The pencil was snapped in half. She held it out to Birdie. "Sorry about your pencil."*

*"It was brand-new." Birdie's lips quivered. "I bought it with my own money."*

*"Tell you what." Sylvia sat beside Birdie. "I'll get you another one when my aunt pays me on Friday." She stroked Birdie's hair.*

*Harry knelt in front of Birdie and tenderly wiped the dirt from her knees and hands. "I need to get these splinters out."*

*Birdie grimaced. "Please don't use a needle."*

"Well, you lucked out. I don't have one in this first-aid kit, only tweezers. Those should be enough."

Harry looked at the bruise on Birdie's head, wishing he had ice to stop the swelling. He set the handkerchief aside and found the tweezers, a box of bandages, cotton balls, and a small bottle of antiseptic. He couldn't take his eyes off the broken pencil in Birdie's hand and her composition book, now splattered with the man's coffee.

"What were you writing out there, Birdie?" Sylvia asked. Harry guessed she wanted to distract her from the tweezers and antiseptic.

"A story about one of the servicemen I met in the canteen line today. His name is Andy. He has a sweetheart named Doris and plans to marry her when he gets home. They almost eloped before he shipped off, but Doris wants a proper wedding. So I wrote their proposal scene."

Sylvia held her hand out to Birdie. "Can I read it?"

Birdie opened her composition book and gave it to Sylvia. "Sure."

Harry found three big splinters in Birdie's knee. The other was scraped up from hitting the platform. "Hold still while I get these splinters out."

He removed them as gently as he could.

Mitch came down the hall. "I'll be right back with your mom, Birdie."

She nodded.

Harry soaked a cotton ball with antiseptic. "Thank you, Mitch." He dabbed the cotton ball on Birdie's knees. She flinched by didn't cry out. If only he had some candy to give her for being so brave, or some change to buy her a soft drink from the machine outside. He placed bandages over her knees then tended to her skinned hands. There was so much he wanted to tell Birdie—how sorry he was for not insisting she finish her story in the waiting area where she would be safe, how guilty he felt that the man came back because he didn't tell Miss Eileen about him stealing from the canteen—but nothing came out.

He shut the first-aid kit. "There you go. You're good as new."

Sylvia closed the notebook, leaving one finger inside as a marker. "You were a brave patient."

Birdie examined her palms. "Thanks."

Sylvia held Birdie's composition book out to Harry. "This is a really good story. You should read it."

Harry set aside the first-aid kit and took the notebook from Sylvia. He opened it to the proposal scene that she'd been reading. It was like something out of a drippy movie with a lot of crying and expressions of unending love. But the fact that ten-year-old Birdie had written it amazed him. "You're an excellent writer, Birdie."

She looked up at him. "Excellent for real, or excellent for a ten-year-old?"

"Excellent for real."

Miss Eileen poked her head out of her office. "Birdie, honey, are you doing okay?"

"Yes, ma'am."

Sylvia got up off the bench. "How about if I get you a drink of water?"

"Yes, please."

Harry remembered an oatmeal cookie in his lunch box. "Do you like oatmeal cookies?"

Birdie nodded.

Harry called to Sylvia, "There's a cookie in my lunchbox. Can you get it for her, please? I'll wait here with her."

Sylvia waved. "Sure thing, Harry."

He handed the book back to Birdie. "You're quite talented."

"My teacher calls my stories 'very creative.' But I can tell by the look on her face it isn't a compliment."

"Well, Sylvia and I think they're great."

Harry's stomach tightened. He tried to guess what Miss Eileen would say to Birdie's mom. Regret overtook him again—and the need to make things right. To do something to make up for the scratched camera and coffee-stained composition book and broken pencil that Birdie had bought with her own money. But I don't have anything to give her. Lord, show me what to do.

*He thought about his fountain pen and the time he let Birdie use it to write her name and how happy it made her. Before Miss Eileen or Sylvia or anyone else came into the room, he reached into his breast pocket and pulled out the pen.*

You're a good man.

*If that medic had seen him let the man in the cap get away with stealing...* Lord, I don't feel like a good man right now.

*He held the pen out to Birdie. "I want you to have this."*

*Sylvia walked in as Birdie took it out of his hand. He heard Sylvia gasp and say, "Harry."*

*Birdie's eyes lit up. "Really?"*

*He nodded. "Really. It's yours." His only regret was that he wouldn't be able to write his next note to Sylvia with it.*

*The awed expression on Birdie's face erased all doubt that Harry had done the right thing by giving it to her.*

Birdie threw her arms around Harry. "Thank you, thank you, thank you."

"A writer should have a fountain pen, not a pencil." He patted her back. "Put it in your pocket so it doesn't get lost."

"Good idea." Birdie slipped it into the pocket of her blazer.

Sylvia handed Birdie the cookie and cup of water. Her eyes remained fixed on Harry.

Harry's attention was torn between Sylvia's shock and Birdie's gratitude. He turned to another story in Birdie's notebook. She'd written one about the man in the red cap. Harry read it and once again remembered the man wolfing down a sandwich. She'd given him a name. John. And a family that depended on his "acts of panhandling for their very survival." He bit his lip to keep from laughing over acts of panhandling. "I hope you keep writing stories like this."

"I will." Birdie put her hand on Harry's arm. "Harry, I need to tell you—"

The sound of someone bursting through the entrance to the depot cut her off. A woman who looked like a grown version of Birdie rushed over and took her by the hand. "Birdie, are you all right?"

Birdie flinched from the obvious pain in her injured palm and tried to pull back. "I'm fine."

Harry handed over Birdie's composition book and stood up, preparing to explain what happened, take full responsibility, and endure the tongue-lashing he felt he had earned.

But Birdie's mom didn't seem to see him or Sylvia. She whisked Birdie away without saying a word to either of them. Harry wanted to tell Birdie's mom how sorry he was, but she left too quickly for him to say even that.

By the time Miss Eileen came out of her office, Birdie and her mother were gone. She looked at Harry and Sylvia. "Thank you both so much for taking care of her."

All Harry could do was nod. After Miss Eileen went back into her office, he felt glued to the depot bench. Sylvia sat beside him.

"Harry, you gave Birdie your fountain pen."

He moved the first-aid kit to his lap. "I wanted to make up for what happened."

"But your fountain pen? She's a ten-year-old girl."

"I know. I felt like she needed it." He looked up at her. "Sylvia, I feel terrible about today. What if that man had kidnapped her or hurt her worse than he did?"

Sylvia inched a little closer to him. "Birdie's going to be okay. Miss Eileen called the police. And look,

*God worked things out. We were both here, and Mitch and Miss Eileen were around to help."*

"If I had told Miss Eileen right away about seeing that man, he wouldn't have come today and hurt Birdie."

"You don't know that for sure."

As nice as that was for Sylvia to say, Harry wasn't convinced. "I didn't even get to tell her or her mom how sorry I am that this happened at all."

"I'm sure they both know. You were so kind to Birdie just now. I'm sure that said everything."

"It's not the same as hearing 'I'm sorry.'"

Sylvia put her hand on Harry's. "You can tell Birdie when she comes back."

# CHAPTER TWENTY-ONE

*J*anet saw Kim outside the café door as Debbie closed her laptop, following a successful meal-planning session. Kim came in with an armload of records and set the pile in front of Debbie.

"Voilà. We have music for your party. Sorry I'm late."

Janet started thumbing through the pile. "Your timing is perfect. We just nailed down the menu. Since Kate wants a formal event and this is a diner and we know our guests aren't into gourmet food, we're serving comfort food with such a fine presentation that she won't notice she's eating homestyle roast beef and mashed potatoes." They'd agreed that would go the furthest and also keep the cost lower for their generous benefactress, Roberta. "For those who don't eat red meat, we have chicken as a choice."

Kim pulled up a chair. "You two could make burgers and fries taste like fine dining."

Janet spotted an Andrews Sisters album and held it up. She rocked it from side to side and belted out the chorus from "Ac-Cent-Tchu-Ate the Positive." She set it aside. "I need a little help applying those lyrics today."

"Uh-oh." Kim moved the rest of her records toward Debbie. "What's going on?"

Janet considered how to answer without resorting to gossip about Kate. "Let's just say I'm struggling with conflicted emotions regarding an otherwise good person who accused one of our most loyal and trusted customers of stealing the fountain pen."

Kim sat down. "Which customer?"

Debbie moved her laptop to the counter. "Harry. The nicest person on the planet."

"You're not serious. Who would do that? On second thought, don't tell me. I'll be way too upset with whoever it is."

"Wise choice. I'm determined to find it, but I haven't known where to begin when it comes to looking outside the café and the depot." Janet went back to sorting through Kim's selection of records. "On the way home today, I plan to check a few local pawn shops."

Kim put her elbow on the table and rested her chin in her hand. "I looked for it online last night. No luck. Did you ever report the theft to the police department?"

"Not yet. I have all the information I need to do that. But whenever I think about making an official report, something stops me. It's Harry I'm most concerned about. He knows that this person I mentioned suspects him."

Debbie took a pad of sticky notes out of her pocket. "But he also knows that the most important people in his life know he didn't take it." She wrote *For Party* on one of the notes and stuck it to the Andrews Sisters album.

Kim picked up a Bing Crosby record. "What upsets me most is that *anyone* took it while the two of you were serving them food."

Janet thought of Harry, who'd given his fountain pen to a little girl who, in his opinion, needed it more than he did. "If Harry wasn't feeling so bad about someone he admires pointing the finger at him, I have a feeling he'd suggest that the person who has the pen now didn't take it to be malicious. That they have it because they need it. If only my thoughts could be that gracious."

On her way home from the café, Janet stopped at the first pawn shop of the three she'd found online that were anywhere nearby. Walking into Brad's Pawn Shop felt nothing like her experiences entering the cozy ambiance of Aunt Maggie's Antiques and Consignment. Brad's smelled like old packing boxes and cigarette smoke. The window display featured an electric guitar, a mountain bike, and power tools. Musical instruments and sporting gear lined every wall. Seeing the center aisles spattered with everything from a snowblower to boxes of old DVDs reminded Janet that when one is desperate for money, they'll sell just about anything. She searched a row of glass cases filled with diamond rings, watches, and coin collections.

A bulky man in faded jeans and a plaid shirt approached Janet while chugging the last of a can of cola. "Can I help you?" He put his fist over his mouth to cover a burp and tossed his can into a plastic-lined box filled with crushed cardboard and fragments of bubble wrap.

"I hope so." Janet took her phone out of her pocket and pulled up the picture of her fountain pen. "By any chance, has anyone come in to pawn or sell this fountain pen?" She laid her phone in front of Brad.

He put on a pair of readers and leaned over the phone. "This isn't the kind of thing I typically get in here. Sorry. If you're looking to buy a fountain pen, I'd try online."

"Actually, this is—was—my fountain pen. It disappeared out of the blue, and I have reason to believe it might have been stolen."

"Are you local?"

"Yes. I co-own the Whistle Stop Café at the old Dennison Station. It was taken from the café."

Brad shrugged. "I'm no detective, but based on what I've learned from running this place, it would be considered pretty stupid for a thief to pawn his stolen goods locally."

Janet took her phone back, feeling deflated. "I never considered that."

"It's most likely being sold online. Or it could be in a pawn shop or flea market a hundred miles from here. Either way, you're most likely in for one of those needle-in-a-haystack searches."

Janet took one more look inside the case, hoping to have her pen magically appear. "Thank you."

"If you want to leave your phone number, I can call you if it turns up."

"That would be great." She dug through her tote bag for her wallet and took out a business card. "I appreciate your help."

Outside, she blew her disappointment and the odors of the pawn shop out through pursed lips. The idea of getting the same answer from two more pawn shop owners prompted her to go home rather than to the next place on her list.

Janet filled Patricia and Debbie in on her disheartening visit to the pawn shop the next morning. "Ian didn't completely agree with the point about thieves not selling to local pawn shops, but after searching online together, we finally had to accept that the needle-in-a-haystack analogy might apply to this situation."

Patricia finished off her morning mocha. "Don't lose heart. I lost the diamond from my favorite necklace once while I was rearranging furniture in the living room. Two weeks later, I found it under a couch cushion that I'd lifted at least ten times during my frantic search. When I finally saw my diamond glistening in the sunlight, I was about to suck it up with the vacuum cleaner."

"That does give me hope, Patricia. Thank you."

Harry came into the café as Patricia was putting on her coat to leave and Janet was about to return to the kitchen. He had a youthful bounce in his step and a blue folder tucked under his arm. He stopped to say hi to his granddaughter.

"Glad I caught you, Patricia. I have a little something for you and my two favorite café owners."

Janet stopped midstride and spun around to greet Harry.

Crosby stood at his side, looking forlorn.

Harry opened the folder and took out some papers. "I have a copy for each of you," he said.

"Is that what I think it is?" Janet went over to take the pages that Harry held out to her and read the top sheet. "'A Girl Named Birdie.'" She reached out and hugged him. "It is."

Harry hugged her back. "I wanted you, Debbie, and Patricia to read it before I turn it in for the anthology."

Janet clapped her hands. "Yay!"

Debbie cleared away Patricia's empty mug and plate, "Woo-hoo!"

Harry gave Debbie's copy to Janet. "Don't read it until I leave."

Patricia playfully smacked his arm with her copy of the story. "Pop Pop, it's going to be in a book. Lots of people will read it."

He stuck out his bottom lip. "I can't help it. I'm an insecure artist."

Janet set the copies on the counter behind her. "You have my word. I'll read it at home before Ian gets off work."

Patricia kissed his cheek. "You have my word too." She slipped her copy of the story into her tote bag.

Harry tightened his grip on Crosby's leash. "Now I'm off to take this guy to the v-e-t."

Crosby let out a whimper.

Harry ushered him to the door. "Oh, now, don't give me that pouty look. It's just your yearly boosters. I'm trying to keep you healthy so you can grow old and gray like me."

Janet waved goodbye. "Good luck, Crosby. If you're a good boy, maybe you'll get a lollipop."

Debbie put Patricia's dishes in a bin. "Or a sticker."

Harry waved and shut the door.

Patricia picked up her tote bag. "How can I follow up that comedy routine? See you tomorrow, ladies."

Janet grabbed a cloth to wipe down the counter. "Have a great day, Patricia."

On her way out, Patricia held the door for an incoming customer.

Janet hung the cloth on a hook on her way to the kitchen. "Feel free to sit anywhere. I'll be right with you." When she turned around, Kate and Roberta waved to her and made their way to Roberta's favorite table by the window.

A half hour later, Kate and Roberta were still seated at the table and lost in a quiet conversation that appeared serious based on the number of times Janet peeked through the kitchen doors and saw either Kate looking down and wiping her eyes or Roberta reaching out to touch her hand.

Staying focused on cooking felt nearly impossible.

Debbie came up behind her as she was cleaning the frying surface after a grilled cheese and patty melt order. "I wonder what's going on out there. I'm not used to seeing Kate look so fragile."

"I know. It's kind of sad, even after being upset with her."

Debbie picked up a carafe of hot water. "I need to offer them refills for their tea, but I don't want to intrude on what is obviously a private moment."

Janet wiped her hands and reached for the carafe. "I'll do it."

But when she nudged the kitchen door open, she saw Roberta take Kate's hand. The only other customers were a couple deciding what to get from the bakery case, so Janet had to work hard not to tune out the snippets of Kate and Roberta's conversation that she could hear from the counter. Kate sounded on the verge of tears over some bills that she could no longer ignore. One had been turned over to collections. Her soon-to-be ex-husband was responsible for half, but with legal costs related to the divorce, even half was more than she could deal with.

"I have to find a job." Kate reached for a napkin and dabbed at the corners of her eyes. "I don't even know where to start."

Janet put the carafe down. They needed space more than a tea warm-up.

Out of the corner of her eye, Janet saw Roberta reach into her purse, set an envelope on the table, and push it across to Kate.

"I want to help."

"Roberta, no. I didn't involve you because I wanted money."

"I planned to give you this before you told me about the bills."

Kate picked up the envelope. Janet returned her attention to the bakery customers, who'd finally decided on two doughnuts and coffees with cream.

She saw Kate start to take cash out of the envelope then push it back in and shake her head. "This is too much."

"Don't be silly," Roberta said.

Kate covered her face with one hand and held the envelope to her chest with the other. Janet averted her eyes and tried to erase the image of the cash poking out of the envelope in Kate's hand and stop her mind from guessing where Roberta might have gotten the money.

# CHAPTER TWENTY-TWO

*April 30, 1945*

"What do you mean you were with your friends?" Mama threw her coat over the arm of the couch. She never threw things. "You were supposed to be with your sister. You know the rules, Margaret. You are in charge of Birdie from the time you both get home from school until supper."

Birdie examined the perfectly straight bandages on her knees. Bruises had formed under the skinned pads of her hands. She imagined a reporter coming to the house to interview her. Maybe she and Harry and Sylvia would get their pictures in the newspaper. Kids at school would see it and stop thinking she was strange.

Her vision of becoming a local celebrity and Harry receiving a special award for being a hero evaporated at the sound of her sister saying her name in a tone that would not impress local reporters at all.

"Birdie isn't completely innocent. She should know better than to go the train station without me." Maggie sank into Dad's favorite recliner. "I'm not the only one who breaks the rules. She interviews the soldiers while they're in line at the canteen. And she takes pictures of them. You said no socializing with the servicemen other than handing out food, thanking them for their service, and wishing them a safe trip. That should apply to both of us, not just me."

"Margaret." Birdie's mother sounded like she might cry at any moment. "This isn't about taking pictures or writing stories. It's about you running off with your friend and leaving your sister to fend for herself."

As mad as Birdie was at Maggie for trying to get her in trouble by tattling about her interviews, she also wanted to reassure her mother that the train station was perfectly safe. "I wasn't by myself, Mama. Harry Franklin was there, and Sylvia, one of the mechanics, and Miss Eileen. I was fine until that man showed up. Besides, I'm old enough to be on my own after school. I'm almost eleven."

"That isn't the point, Roberta. Do you have any idea what could have happened if that porter hadn't heard you?" Mama's eyes were red from crying and worrying. She pointed to her bedroom. "Your father is in there wounded from the war, trying to recover so he can at least work again. Ruby is on the other side of the world, nursing injured and dying servicemen. I don't need to also be worrying about the two of you being in harm's way. From now on, the canteen is forbidden. The only time you're allowed at the Dennison Station is if we are boarding a train as a family."

"But Mother." Maggie lowered her gaze, and Birdie knew she was trying to appear remorseful and inno-cent. "What about our contribution to the war effort?"

Mama shook a scolding finger in Maggie's direction. "If you wanted to contribute to the war effort, why were you with your friends all afternoon? If your concern was for the soldiers, you would have gone to the canteen after bringing the groceries home. You didn't even get everything on my list." She took a handkerchief from her apron pocket and wiped her eyes. "You can find another way to sup-port the war. Something that doesn't involve being at the train station."

Birdie felt a big lump rising in her throat. She tried to swallow it down like she had when she fell on the platform and her head hit the lamp post and when Harry pulled out her splinters and put antiseptic on her knees. This time she failed. "I have to go back to the station. I need to thank Harry for saving me from that man. And I need to tell him something."

"I'm sure he knows how grateful you are. I don't want to hear another word about it."

Harry's fountain pen poked Birdie's arm from inside her blazer pocket. She put her hand over it. Maybe if her mother saw what a nice gift Harry gave her, she would know what a good friend Harry was. She would surely let her go back to the station one more time.

Or Mama might take the pen away. She might insist on returning it to Harry. She would take it to Dennison Station herself.

Birdie saw Maggie pouting on Dad's favorite chair. She wanted to yell at her, "This is all your fault. I'll never see my friend Harry again because of you. I'll never write another soldier interview."

But in her heart, she knew the truth. That what happened with the man in the cap was her own fault. She had a picture in her camera to prove it.

Later, Birdie stared up at the ceiling in the bedroom she shared with Maggie and wiped her eyes with her sleeve. Her blazer lay tossed at the foot of her bed, over her extra quilt. She kicked it off. Her head hurt.

*Her knees and hands stung. But her heart hurt more than anything. She clutched Harry's beautiful fountain pen in her fist. She could hear her mother and Maggie in the living room—Maggie crying, Mother saying her theatrics would not change a thing. Then she heard the sound of Dad hobbling into the living room supported by his crutches. Maggie's in for it now. After that, all Birdie heard was a lot of mumbling from her parents and a weepy "I'm sorry" from Maggie.*

*Just when Birdie was about to get up and find a good hiding place for her pen, she heard Maggie's saddle shoes hitting the wooden floor of the hallway leading to their room. She rolled over on her side to face the wall. She heard her sister come in, shut the door, and flop onto her bed on the other side of the room.*

*Maggie sniffed hard and let out a pitiful sob. "It's your turn to set the table."*

*"In a minute." Birdie tightened her grip around the pen and rolled onto her back again, keeping her hand hidden between her body and the wall.*

*She expected Maggie to start carrying on about whose fault it was that they couldn't go back to the train station—and she knew who her big sister would blame. Birdie got ready to fight back. Maggie sat on the edge of her bed with her arms folded, her eyes on Birdie. Just when Birdie was about to snap, "Stop staring at me and say something,"* Maggie came to sit beside her. She ran her fingers gently over the bruise on Birdie's forehead and the bandages on her knees.

"I'm sorry, Birdie." She sounded truly sorry. Not just sorry because she got into trouble.

Birdie's throat tightened. "It's okay."

"No, it's not. I shouldn't have left you. Something terrible could have happened to you." Maggie's voice cracked. "Please forgive me."

Birdie tucked the pen under herself and sat up. "You were really mean today."

"I know. I was awful. If it makes you feel any better, I'm grounded until further notice and can't go to the dance on Friday."

Birdie ran her hands over her knees. Maggie's restriction would have made her feel a lot better if she didn't feel as if she'd been punished too. No more interviews with service members at the Salvation Army canteen. No more Saturdays watching trains come and go. No more Harry, the only person who didn't think she was a "very creative" pest who asked too many questions.

She thought about how nice he and Sylvia and Miss Eileen had been to her after the man in the red cap grabbed her camera. Harry would want her to forgive Maggie. So would Sylvia. "Yeah, I forgive you."

"Thanks." Maggie touched Birdie's bruise again. "Does it still hurt?"

"Kind of."

"You should be more careful. Around strangers, I mean."

"You aren't careful when you flirt at the canteen."

Maggie sniffled again. "I suppose I deserve that. And just so you know, I didn't write my name and address in any of those magazines at the canteen. I wanted to. But I knew Mother would ground me for the rest of my life if I started getting letters from a soldier who isn't family."

Birdie patted her sister's leg. "There's hope for you yet, Margaret Constance."

Maggie elbowed her, in a fun way, not like when she was mad. "Oh, go set the table, Roberta Louise."

Birdie reached under her leg for her pen. She started sliding toward the end of her bed, thinking about how to slip the pen under the quilt without Maggie noticing.

"What are you hiding in your hand?"

Birdie sat motionless with the pen halfway under the quilt.

"Whatever it is, I won't take it." Maggie's voice softened. "I promise."

*Birdie scooted over to where her sister sat and slowly opened her fist, revealing the beautiful pen. "Harry Franklin gave it to me today." Knowing she might not ever see him again made her want to bury her face in her pillow and cry.*

*"He gave you that?"*

*"Yes. I think he felt bad because the man in the cap broke my pencil and splashed coffee on my composition book."*

*She waited for her sister to accuse her of taking the pen or suggest that it was inappropriate for her to take a gift from Harry. Instead, she said, "That's a nice pen."*

*Birdie ran her fingers over the smooth, pearly, copper-colored surface. "He and his friend Sylvia liked my stories. He thinks I'm a good writer."*

*"Is that what you've been writing in that composition book?"*

*"Yes. After I interview the soldiers, I write stories about them."*

*"I thought you were just playing reporter like a goofy little kid."*

*"Roberta," Mama shouted from the kitchen, "please come set the table."*

*"Coming!" Birdie looked at the pen and let out a long sigh as dramatic as one of Maggie's. "I'm afraid*

Mama will take this away if she sees it. She'll say it's not suitable for a girl my age."

"She's upset right now, but she'll calm down." Maggie got up and went to the desk where they took turns doing homework. She picked up the wooden lap desk that once belonged to their grandma. It was where they kept their school supplies and sheets of V-Mail for writing letters to Ruby, and to Dad before he got injured. "How about if we put it in here for now? When Mama is feeling better, you can explain." Maggie opened the lid of the desk. "You can use the pen to write letters to Ruby and maybe some of the boys we know who are overseas. I bet your letters will be better than mine."

Birdie tucked her treasured fountain pen behind a stack of V-mail sheets and closed the lap desk. She looked up at her big sister and almost started crying again.

Maggie put her arms around Birdie for the first time in months. "I'm so glad you're okay. I'm sure you'll be able to see Harry again. Maybe after Mama gets some rest, she'll have a change of heart."

Birdie buried her face against her sister's shoulder. "I hope so." She needed to tell him the truth about what happened.

# CHAPTER TWENTY-THREE

T his whole situation is so weird." Janet reached for a bowl of risen bread dough and turned it over on her floured work surface while Debbie helped her out by prepping a batch of pancake batter. "When I heard about Kate's financial issues and considered how quickly she wanted me to suspect Harry, I wondered if she might be the thief. I let my mind go there because I was mad at her. It felt natural to wonder about Roberta after learning that Harry gave her the pen, until I came back to the fact that she seems way too nice to steal even if the pen did once belong to her. But when I saw her and Kate together yesterday, my heart sank."

Debbie reached for a giant whisk. "I know. When you told me about their cash exchange, my mind went in the same direction."

Janet started breaking off small lumps of dough for sticky buns. "She said she would do anything for dear Kate. And if they are close friends, she would know that Kate's brother-in-law is a pen collector."

Debbie whipped the batter with impressive speed. "I started wondering if they were in on it together until you told me how Kate reacted to the money."

"Same here." Janet placed three balls into a generously buttered muffin tin. The thought that nagged at her while discussing this whole thing with Ian the night before wouldn't let go. "I don't want to be like Kate, making assumptions about a person I don't know based on superficial details."

Debbie tapped her whisk on the side of the mixing bowl. "Except in this case, those superficial details might add up to something. Kate and Roberta were both in the café when the pen went missing. Kate is buried in debt. And if Roberta owned the pen after Harry did, she might have known its value."

"If she didn't know before, she found out when Kim stopped by to show us what she saw on that collector's site. In the chaos of the past week or so, I can't remember if I told you this or not, but when I brought her meal to the table, she was jotting something down in a notebook."

Debbie looked up at the ceiling then at Janet. "Then she suddenly had to take her lunch to go."

"And she just happened to show up to join Kate and her grandmother for tea the next day when the pen disappeared." Janet checked the clock. The café opened in an hour, and the sticky buns still needed to rise for thirty and bake for another thirty. She sped up her tin-filling process.

Debbie washed her hands and joined the dough-ball-rolling race with the clock. "Now that we're talking through this together, I understand why you feel so confused and conflicted. I'm starting to feel the exact same way. If those details pointed to a shifty stranger who came to the café when the pen disappeared, I would think, yay, we have the answer. But when they point to a sweet old lady who wrote a cute note to Harry and her possibly selling it to the brother-in-law of someone I used to go to church with, it gets more complicated."

"One thing I've learned through this whole experience with Kate's workshop is that people can be extremely complicated." Janet covered the tin of lovely clusters of dough balls and reached for a bowl to start the syrup. "I better stop thinking about this for now and concentrate on us opening for the day. If I keep obsessing, we might end up with balls of raw bread dough in the bakery case instead of sticky buns."

"Or run the risk of you interrogating Roberta the minute she pops in for tea at her favorite table by the window."

"Both would be equally embarrassing." She went to the pantry to get the brown sugar and cinnamon. "On a brighter note, did you read Harry's story?"

Debbie's eyes got a melancholy glint in them. "Yes."

"Did you cry?"

"Yes!" Debbie set the bowl of batter aside. "I know you've probably been bound by some kind of confidentiality agreement, but I just have to ask. Am I correct in thinking Roberta and Birdie are the same person?"

"Yep. You guessed correctly."

"That does take the complication of this to a new level. As if being blamed for stealing his own pen isn't enough, I can't imagine how sad Harry will feel if the little girl who used to follow him around like a puppy took it."

***

Patricia entered the café before anyone else and made herself at home on the stool closest to the bakery case. Before Janet had a chance to greet her, Patricia pulled out her copy of Harry's story. "In case you haven't read this yet, Pop-Pop can really write."

"Isn't it sweet?" She was tempted to tell Patricia about Harry's original motivation for writing the story, but she held back. "I must admit, as frustrating as it was to feel pressured into helping with the writing workshop, it's so fun to be part of it now. Harry could write a book."

"That's what I told him last night when he called to ask me to be his date for the celebration dinner."

Janet got a plate and mug for Patricia's daily peppermint mocha and whatever sweet treat she wanted. Harry and Crosby arrived as she was pouring frothed milk over the espresso, chocolate, and peppermint syrup.

Debbie met him at the door. "Why, hello there, Mr. Hemingway. You're here bright and early."

Janet shut off the milk frother. "It isn't even a workshop day."

Harry paused at the writing station. "I thought I'd stop by to say hello and have coffee with my granddaughter before heading to Good Shepherd. Eileen and Ray and I getting together to give each other feedback on our stories before turning them in to Kate."

Patricia got up from her stool and moved her coat and tote bag to the nearest table. "What a fun surprise." She crouched down to say hello to Crosby. "Hey, Crosby. Have you recovered from your vet visit?"

Harry pulled out a chair for Patricia. "He put up a fuss on the drive over, but in the end, he handled it like a trouper."

Janet put the finishing touches on Patricia's drink. "So, I have some feedback on your story."

Harry looked around the empty dining area. "Give it to me straight while it's only the four of us in here."

Janet delivered Patricia's mocha. "First, what can I get you?"

"Just a regular cup of joe and a cinnamon roll." Harry unclipped Crosby's leash. "Are you putting off telling me I should stick to watching trains?"

Debbie picked up the pot of freshly brewed coffee. "Not at all."

Janet hurried to get the cinnamon roll before more customers arrived. "Harry, your story is wonderful. The three of us were just talking about how much we loved it."

Debbie poured him a cup of coffee and brought it to him. "Your coffee and cinnamon roll are on the house. That's how good your story was."

Patricia smiled at him. "I got to see you and Grandma Sylvia as teenagers. And now I know who you gave your fountain pen to. You were kind beyond words even as a young man."

"I wrote my first note to Sylvia with that fountain pen. An invitation to a youth picnic at church."

Patricia seemed to have forgotten all about her morning pastry. "Grandma showed me that note when I was a little girl. She kept it all those years."

"I still can't believe she did that." Harry held his fork over his cinnamon roll. "I fell in love with her the minute I saw her standing in front of the train schedule board with her toolbox in her hand and her hair tied up in a red-and-white checked scarf. Man, she was pretty."

Patricia nudged Harry. "She thought you were pretty handsome too."

"Not like her." He cut into his roll. "She had the most beautiful smile I've ever seen."

Patricia's eyes glistened. "She had the best smile."

Janet felt tears coming to her eyes too. She hadn't known Sylvia Franklin well, but she vividly remembered the beautiful smile.

Harry pointed to his teeth. "And those teeth. So white and straight."

Patricia sent a tearful glance Janet's way. "I was always jealous of her perfect teeth. Mine didn't even look that good after braces."

Janet went to get one of the fresh sticky buns out of the bakery case as a surprise for Patricia.

Harry took a bite of his roll and stared at the window overlooking the place where trains once passed almost hourly. "Sylvia and I had our first kiss on May eighth, nineteen forty-five. I remember the date because it was V-E Day." He pointed to the window with his fork. "Right out there in front of God and everybody. Eileen and the other porter on duty and everyone at the canteen was hugging and crying over the news, so I doubt we stood out for our public display of affection. But we felt like we were the only ones on the planet. I knew at that moment that I was going to marry Sylvia McCurdy."

Janet set the sticky bun in front of Patricia. "So when are you going to write that story?"

"Maybe when I get home today. It's too late to get it ready for the anthology, but I'll write it just for you, Patricia. And for Janet and Debbie."

Patricia ran her spoon around the inside of her mug to release the whipped cream. "I have one question about the story you wrote about Birdie. You ended it with an apology to her, which was really nice. But I think Grandma Sylvia would say you're being a little too hard on yourself. You were only a teenager when the man in the red cap started hanging around the train station. When I was that age, if I'd seen a man steal food because he was starving, I might have let it slide too. Not that being hungry made it right, but you were just a kid in a tough situation."

Debbie stood behind Harry and put her hand on his shoulder. "I agree, Harry. I have a feeling that Birdie would say the same thing if she were standing here right now."

Harry took a bite of his roll and swallowed before speaking. "I think I knew that deep down, the more I had time to think about it, but when I met Roberta and realized she was Birdie all grown up, I saw this as my chance to give her the apology I wanted to give back then."

Patricia picked up her mug. "Who's Roberta?"

Janet sat down between Harry and Patricia. "Remember that white-haired woman who came in the day I set up the writing station?"

Harry added, "The one you ladies thought wanted to ask me out on a date?"

Patricia gaped at them. "That was Birdie?" she finally squeaked out.

"That's her," her grandfather said. "She's been helping with the writing workshop."

"So she wasn't staring at you to flirt. She was staring because she recognized you." Patricia narrowed her big brown eyes then gave her grandfather a look of loving concern. "Did she bring up what happened? Is that why you felt the need to apologize?"

Harry pulled his cinnamon roll closer. "She never has. In fact, she's been nothing but friendly and encouraging. But you know how it is when you sense God saying, 'It's time to clear the air. This is your chance'? That's how I felt when I got the idea for this story. Birdie returned to the train station. It just took her a lot longer than I expected."

The door to the café opened, and Debbie went over to greet the customers.

Patricia reached for her coffee. "You know, Pop Pop, now that you have the story off your chest, you could always ask Roberta why she never returned. You might find out it had nothing to do with you."

Janet stood up to go back to work, suddenly feeling sad over the possibility that Harry's old friend could be the thief.

# CHAPTER TWENTY-FOUR

*May 5, 1945*

*"Have you seen Birdie today?"*

*Miss Eileen shut the gate between the platform and the train tracks. "No, Harry. I haven't seen her around here for a few days."*

*Harry tried to stop looking at the bench where Birdie so often sat with her composition book and camera waiting for the next train to arrive so she could interview soldiers. "I haven't seen her since Monday." Even almost a week later, he felt the sting of what had happened to Birdie. Miss Eileen had given him a lecture after he confessed to seeing the man in the red cap steal from the canteen and keeping quiet about it. He was thankful to still have his job after disobeying her, and even more grateful to know the man had been arrested.*

Miss Eileen greeted a pair of canteen volunteers coming through with a crate of apples and two big loaves of bread. "Come to think of it, I haven't seen her sister here either. I would know her anywhere. She passes out as many winks and flirtatious smiles as sandwiches and doughnuts."

The empty bench looked lonely without Birdie. "I hope Birdie's okay." Maybe the bump on her head was worse than he and Sylvia had thought. Or maybe she was afraid to come to the depot after such a frightening experience.

"Her family could be busy this weekend."

"I suppose so." Harry held the door to the depot open for Miss Eileen and followed her inside. "I hope she comes back soon. I owe her an apology for what happened."

"She'll be back."

Sylvia opened the door to the waiting area and peeked inside. "I'm heading home, Harry. See you later."

"Bye, Sylvia."

"See you tonight?"

"I'll pick you up at seven."

Miss Eileen waved goodbye to Sylvia and gave Harry a sly grin. "And what was that about, Mr. Franklin?"

"I'm taking Sylvia to see the new Laurel and Hardy movie tonight. Our first real date that isn't a church event."

"I'm happy for you, Harry. Sylvia is a lovely young lady."

"Yes, ma'am. She sure is." His eyes drifted to the bench at the front of the waiting area where he and Sylvia tended to Birdie. He couldn't wait to see Birdie's face when she learned he finally found a sweetheart.

# CHAPTER TWENTY-FIVE

ebbie locked the door to the café. "If we divide and conquer this afternoon, we can get everything else we need for the dinner. My mom has a bunch of candles and vintage holders, so I'll get those from her, and you can pick up the tablecloths that Charla is lending us."

Janet zipped up her coat. "Then I'm heading to the thrift store to see if I can find something that resembles chefs' outfits. It was Charla's idea, so she offered to pay for them."

"We aren't going to argue with that."

Kim came out of the museum with her coat and purse. "Hey, Janet, before you leave, I have a special request. Kate called to ask if I would be willing to put a few copies of the anthology in the museum gift shop. When you see her on Monday, would you tell her I'll take ten? I hope it's not too late."

"Not at all. Stories are due Wednesday, and she's determined to format them and get the book to the printer on Friday."

"Don't tell anyone from the class though. My plan is to display one in the window of the ticket office the night of the dinner, with a big sign."

Janet took out her key fob. "This event is going to be full of surprises. A speaker who is yet to be revealed, *Our Collective Memory* in the gift shop."

Debbie put on her coat. "Gourmet roast beef and potatoes."

Janet spun her key fob around her finger and caught it in her hand. "And as much as I know Kate would like to see the writing station hidden away for the party, we're keeping it out."

Debbie rattled the doorknob to confirm it was locked and shut tight. "To satisfy her request for a formal setting, we'll string white lights around it."

Kim took out her keys and locked the door to the museum. "Wouldn't it be nice if God surprised you by having your pen turn up?"

Janet led the way to the exit. "At this point in the search, I would consider that a miracle."

After scoring big-time at a thrift store in New Philly, Janet whipped out her phone to call Debbie on her way back to the car. "A couple of people must have given up on culinary school recently. I just found two chef hats and two white double-breasted jackets. All Charla and I need are white aprons, which we both have already, side towels, and if we really want to be authentic, checked pants. But I think we'll go with black slacks."

"Fantastic. Wait. You own black slacks?"

"Very funny." Janet opened her trunk. "Yes, I own black slacks." She only wore them when forced, but she had them. "Did you get the candles?"

"Not only did I get the candles and the vintage holders, but Mom also gave me a bunch of red sparkly plates to set them on and silk flowers to place around them. The tables are going to look gorgeous."

"Sounds festive." Janet found a place in the trunk where the bag containing the hats and jackets wouldn't get crushed.

"Would it be over-the-top to do a drawing for a door prize or two, since it's a party?"

"I think that would be fun. Your mom and Charla loaned us the decorations, and Charla is springing for your chef costumes, so door prizes can be our contribution. I remember seeing some homemade journals at Aunt Maggie's. I'll swing by there before going home."

"Perfect. If she's out of them, don't worry about it. It was a last-minute thought."

Janet opened the driver's side door and hopped into the car. "I'm sure she'll have something suitable. The only thing I'll stay away from is fountain pens."

At Aunt Maggie's, Janet found Anne's husband behind the counter. "Hello again," he said. "I'll let Anne know you're here."

"I don't want to bother her if she's busy. I'm just here to pick up a couple of the homemade journals I saw when I came in the first time."

Rick showed Janet to the table covered with a selection of journals in all sizes. "Take your time. I'm sure she'll be out soon. She and her great-aunt went to the back to find something."

"Will do. Thanks." While browsing the journals, Janet felt more consumed by the reality of Roberta being in the store than the variety of sizes and covers she had to choose from. There was so much she wanted to ask her—about the scene in the café with Kate and her history with Harry.

She decided on a fat journal with a Paris-themed fabric cover and a burgundy faux-leather one with a strap that wound around it and closed with a key that fit into a small pocket. Both were refillable. She lingered a little longer to wait for Anne and Roberta but finally decided to pay and go home. None of her questions for Roberta could be discussed in front of Anne and her husband anyway. She took her purchases to the counter. "Please tell Anne I'm sorry I missed her."

Rick added two pens with the store logo on them to Janet's bag. "I sure will. Still no luck finding the fountain pen?"

"No, unfortunately."

"That's a shame." He handed her the bag just as Anne and Roberta emerged from the back room.

"I thought I heard your voice." Anne came over and greeted Janet with a hug. She took Roberta's hand. "Look who finally decided to visit."

Janet extended a hug to Roberta as well. "What do you think of this place?"

"I love it. Maggie would be proud."

Janet took a step back. "I'll let the two of you finish your visit. See you at the next class, Roberta."

"I'm on my way out too, so I'll follow you." She kissed Anne's cheek. "See you and Rick at the celebration dinner?"

Anne took her aunt's hand. "I wouldn't miss it."

Roberta buttoned her coat and adjusted her purse on her shoulder. "These two are my guests."

Anne joined her husband behind the counter. "It will give me a chance to tell the group that I plan to sell copies of the anthology here in the store."

"Harry and Eileen and the others are going to feel like local celebrities," Janet said. "The museum at the depot is taking some too."

"They deserve to feel like celebrities. According to my aunt, we have some pretty amazing stories in that book."

"We do." Janet turned toward the door. "See you next week. I won't say a word."

She expected to part ways with Roberta outside, but the elderly woman stopped outside the shop door instead. "I'm glad I ran into you, Janet. I've been wanting to talk to you."

Janet spotted a coffee shop across the parking lot. "Would you like to grab a cup of tea? My treat."

"I would love to."

As they walked, Janet caught herself picturing Roberta as the little girl Harry had described. She had a hard time imagining the poised, stylish woman beside her being "scrappy," as Roberta put it.

Ten minutes later, Janet blew on her cup of chai tea, suddenly feeling awkward sitting across from the woman who used to be a little girl named Birdie.

Roberta bobbed her tea bag in her cup and broke the silence. "I've been meaning to talk to you about Kate accusing Harry of taking your fountain pen."

"You know about that?"

Roberta nodded. "She came to me with the same crazy idea. I shut her down immediately." She removed her tea bag. "Kate is going through a lot right now. She isn't herself."

"I know. I mean…I saw her looking sad when the two of you were at the café last week."

"Yes, last week was especially hard for her. It's not my place to share details, but I was able to help lighten the burden a bit. When my husband passed, he left me well cared for, and I vowed to share the wealth." Roberta wrapped her hands around her cup. "I just want to assure you that Kate adores Harry. If she hasn't apologized already, she plans to."

Janet took a whiff of the milky chai in front of her. "Roberta, can I ask you something personal?"

"That depends on how personal you plan to get."

Janet detected a hint of playfulness in her tone.

"I read Harry's story about you as a little girl. Do you plan to tell him why you never returned to the depot? He's been carrying around a lot of guilt over what happened to you that day."

"I'm so glad you brought up his story. I read it this morning. I thought I was the only one who felt guilty over what happened that day. So, to answer your question, yes. I do plan to talk to Harry."

"Why do you feel guilty? If I read Harry's story correctly, the man in the red cap attacked you."

"Yes, he did, but… Let's just say I wasn't completely innocent." She reached into her purse and took out a zipper bag of pictures. It looked like the one Janet and Anne had seen earlier. "As I told you, I was a bit too curious for my own good back then. Sometimes it got me into trouble. I'd been warned to stay away from the man in the cap, but that day, all alone out there on the platform waiting for Sylvia to walk me home, I didn't see any harm in taking a picture of him. I can still see him sitting on the edge of the platform, eating a sandwich and drinking his coffee. I'd never seen him look so relaxed. It was a story waiting to be written. I picked up my camara and..." She formed an invisible camera around her eyes with her fingers. "Snap."

"I take it he wasn't happy."

"No." Roberta took two pictures out of the bag and slid them across the table to Janet. "To make matters worse, I walked over with my composition book and pencil and tried to justify my actions by saying, 'I just want to know your story, mister. Where did you get the sandwich? Did someone from the canteen take pity on you?'" She cringed. "I still can't believe I said, 'take pity on you' to a man in his situation."

"You were ten. I might have done something just as insensitive at that age."

"It never occurred to me that someone at the station would think my interviews were anything but adorable. While many of the servicemen thought I was doing a project for school, that man thought I planned to turn him into the police."

"Oh no. That's why he tried to grab your camera."

"That's why. He wasn't after it so he could sell it. He wanted the nosy kid with the notebook and questions to leave him alone."

"That still doesn't make what he did your fault. He could have simply ignored you and left."

"Oh, of course. I know that now. But as a child, I didn't see it that way. Harry was my hero that day. I was so upset when my mother wouldn't let me and my sister go back to the station."

"So that's why you didn't return."

"Mama was furious. Not at Harry. She was mad at my sister Maggie for running off with her friends and leaving me to wander around town by myself. Our dad was recovering from a war injury, and our sister was serving as a nurse in Japan. Mama didn't have the energy to worry about us too. So, from then on, we were forbidden from going to the depot. That summer, my father got a job in Columbus and we moved."

"Birdie… I mean Roberta… Harry needs to know this."

"If I'd known about the guilt he carried all these years, I would have told him before now." She took another sip of her tea, looking thoughtfully over her cup. "I think I know how I want to do it too."

Instead of asking how, as if that was any of her business, Janet offered Roberta a warm smile. "Thanks for telling me what happened."

"Thank you for wanting to know."

"I guess this is a good reminder that two people can see the same story in very different ways."

"That's right. It's also a reminder that there might be a story behind why a person chooses to do something wrong. Kind of like that missing fountain pen of yours."

"What? Do you know who took the fountain pen?"

"I have an idea. That's all I can say at this point."

⁂

That night Janet handed Ian two plates for the table. "Who could she possibly be referring to? Kate maybe?"

Ian set one plate at his spot at the table and the other at Janet's. "I don't know, but it sounds like you might be a step closer to finding out."

"I guess all I can do is wait. Which will drive me a little bit crazy, to be honest."

Ian got two glasses out of the cupboard. "Yeah, instead of solving a crime, you have to leave it to a kind old lady and stick to baking for a while."

# CHAPTER TWENTY-SIX

*A* few days later, on Wednesday morning, in the quiet of the café, Janet opened her Bible app while waiting for the cinnamon rolls to rise. She sat at the table with a cup of coffee and pulled up the verse for the day. "Therefore encourage one another and build each other up, just as in fact you are doing." The familiar words of 1 Thessalonians 5:11 felt like the perfect start to a day that would include her last time of helping in the workshop at Good Shepherd. They had another class on Monday to talk about the publishing process, then the dinner on Wednesday night. She said a prayer for Nora, that she would have her story finished in time. Then she prayed for Kate.

*Lord, I forgive Kate for blaming Harry.*

She got up and went to the writing station to post 1 Thessalonians 5:11 on the message board. She took two cards with envelopes out of the lap desk and wrote *Nora* on one and *Kate* on the other.

A nagging feeling in the pit of her stomach stopped her before she had a chance to write out her verse.

*While I'm on the topic of forgiveness, Lord, Kate isn't the only one who needs some.*

Janet didn't realize she was being quiet until Debbie asked, "What are you thinking about?"

Janet piped a generous layer of icing across a row of cinnamon rolls. "How can you tell I'm not just lost in my work?"

"Because I've known you forever. That's not your lost-in-work expression. It's your thinking-deeply-about-something face."

Janet lifted the piping tube and caught a glob of icing on her fingertips. "I had a rather humbling moment with God before you arrived."

"Oh, one of those. Is it private between you and God, or are you able to share?"

Janet set the piping tube on the table and reached for a paper towel, despite the temptation to lick the icing off her fingers. "I can share. He helped me realize that assuming Kate or Roberta stole the fountain pen because of Kate's financial problems was just as wrong as Kate pointing the finger at Harry because he's old and might have gotten confused." She piped another swirly line of icing. "I thought I was being so holy when I told God I forgave Kate for blaming Harry. Until I recognized my need to ask Him to forgive me for making assumptions about Kate and Roberta."

"Ouch."

"Ouch is right. Yesterday when I had that spontaneous tea with Roberta, I knew immediately that I'd been wrong about her. She's a really nice person who gave a friend money to help her out of a financial hole after already being generous enough to cover the dinner. She didn't share where it came from, and I don't care." Janet stood back to readjust her tray. "Roberta said she has an idea of who took the pen."

"No!"

"And you know what? After my moment with God this morning and realizing how quickly otherwise nice women were willing to blame the first person who did something unusual, I'm leaving it with Him."

Debbie took an apron off the hook beside the refrigerator. "I admire your ability to do that."

"Don't be too impressed. I'm still upset the pen is gone, especially knowing it was most likely Harry's. I really wanted to give it to him. But I'd rather not find it than risk blaming an innocent person."

Debbie finished tying her apron. "Maybe Roberta will end up finding it."

"That would be great. But for now, I'm ready to give up the search. If God wants us to find it, we will."

Janet set her plate of cinnamon rolls on the table in the activities room. She noticed Kate trying to move a round table by herself and ran to her aid. "Let me help you."

Kate stopped and rested her hands on her back. "I appreciate that. Thanks."

Together, they moved the table to the center of the room.

"Where's your gran?"

"She'll be along soon. I think she might finally be making friends. When I arrived this morning, she was chatting with Eileen, so I let her be."

"It's thanks to this class, I'm sure."

"I can't take all the credit. Eileen is pretty irresistible."

"That she is. Between Eileen, Ray, and Harry, she'll never be lonely." Janet started walking back to the refreshments table to uncover her cinnamon rolls.

Kate came up beside her. "I'll stop by the café this afternoon to see how much I owe for the dinner."

The idea of lifting one more financial weight from Kate's shoulders brought a joy to Janet's heart that would have felt out of reach when they first met. "You don't owe anything."

"How is that—"

"All I can say is, people really care about you, Kate."

She pressed her trembling lips together. "This is such a gift from God."

"Because He also cares about you."

"Hey, Janet, I owe you an apology." Kate toyed with a stack of paper cups. "I owe Harry one too, but since it's just the two of us now, I want to start with you. It was wrong of me to blame Harry for taking the pen. Will you forgive me, please? I'm not saying this because of the good news you gave me. It's been weighing on me since yesterday."

Janet turned to look at her only to see that Kate couldn't seem to make eye contact. "I forgive you."

"I read the story about Harry's fountain pen. Then Roberta and I had a long talk about the day he gave it to her." She finally managed to meet Janet's eyes. "I was wrong. I know what it feels like to feel judged. I've promised myself that from now on I'll always assume the best about people when I don't know all the facts."

Janet wanted to tell Kate that she knew what she'd been through. Instead, she reached out and gave her arm a gentle squeeze. "Harry is a very forgiving person."

"Thank you for that." She picked up a napkin and blew her nose. "This is going to sound strange, but when I saw the pen at the café, I felt a strange sense of ownership, like I needed to protect it. Not just because I knew its value. It looked familiar to me."

"Familiar how?"

"I don't know. I feel like I've seen it somewhere. Remember when I told you my brother-in-law took me into an expensive stationery store where I saw a pen like yours? Even then, it looked familiar to me. I had a vague recollection of seeing one like it in an old family photo." She threw away her napkin. "It could be that it was similar to one Lance already had." She ducked her head. "I remember resenting being in that store, seeing him contemplate buying a two-thousand-dollar pen while I was losing everything."

"I'm really sorry about that, Kate."

She took a shaky breath. "I appreciate that, but it was our own fault. Doug and I started cutting corners in our business to save money. We held on to an employee we should have fired months before, because he was a friend's son. Our marriage didn't survive the stress. My list of regrets is far longer than we have time for right now."

Janet stood in silence to avoid the risk of throwing out a pat answer.

"Blaming Harry is one of those regrets. I know for certain he didn't have anything to do with the pen disappearing."

"It'll mean a lot to him to hear that." Janet pulled back the plastic wrap on her plate, sending the aroma of cinnamon and sugar into the room as Eileen and Nora walked in.

"Cinnamon rolls," Nora exclaimed. "My favorite."

"I'm glad. It will make up for all that gingerbread." Janet reached under the table to stash her tote bag. Before standing all the way up, she took two cards out of the side compartment and slipped them into her sweater pocket.

Unlike during other workshop sessions, Kate let everyone use the time to polish their stories. Janet took her usual place at Nora's table. She enjoyed watching how quickly those who were finished with their stories rallied around the others to offer help with proof-reading, formatting, and getting them emailed to Kate.

Nora sat down beside her. She pushed her legal pad across the table. "I have a little gift for you."

As soon Janet saw the printed pages clipped to the pad, she wanted to get up and give Nora a hug. She opted for a less conspicuous thumbs-up. "You did it! I'm so proud of you."

"I still need to email it to Kate. Before I do, I thought I'd see what you think."

Janet crossed one leg over the other and leaned back to read the title. "'Mama's Gingerbread.'"

Nora interrupted her before she got through the first line. "You aren't going to read it right here in front of me, are you?"

When Janet saw the horrified expression on Nora's face, it hit her how difficult it had been for the elderly woman to show her the story at all let alone sit there waiting for her reaction to it. "Tell you what. How about if I go out into the hall to read this and you see if Kate or any of the others need some help?"

Nora hesitated. She looked around the room.

"I bet there's someone in the room who would appreciate your feedback on their story," Janet suggested.

Nora didn't reply, and just when Janet was trying to come up with a second reason for how Nora might benefit the class, Harry said, "Come on over to our table, Nora. Ray is stuck on how to word something."

"Go on," Janet urged when Nora didn't move. She stood up and held Nora's legal pad against her chest. "You'll be great. You used to teach for a living, remember?"

Finally, Nora nodded and put one hand on her walker, "I suppose it'll be easier than sitting here waiting for you to give me an F-minus."

Janet patted Nora's arm. "I'm not going to give you an F-minus. I bet your story is one of the best in the class."

Out in the hallway, Janet wiped away tears while turning the last page of Nora's story. Instead of writing about what she'd learned through her years of being passed from one relative to another, she'd poured out a bittersweet memory of watching her mother bake gingerbread and lovingly pack it into a sack lunch for Nora's father.

*We had gingerbread cookies leftover from Christmas.*
*But Mama wasn't about to give Daddy leftovers. She got up*

*early that morning to make fresh gingerbread for Daddy and packed as much as she could fit into the brown bag with his two sandwiches and an orange, knowing it was his favorite.*

*"He'll have a taste of home during his trip," Mama said.*

*That night after supper, after feeling sad all day because Daddy had to leave so soon after a lovely visit, we ate what was left in the gingerbread pan and said a prayer for Daddy.*

*After Daddy was killed, Mama stopped baking gingerbread.*

*When Mama passed away, gingerbread started tasting like cinnamon sand and made my throat hurt.*

*Then one day, a lady showed up with gingerbread that smelled just like Mama's. I couldn't eat any. I went to her café. More gingerbread. It followed me around for two weeks until I finally took a tiny taste of it.*

*I thought of Daddy.*

*I thought of Mama.*

*I cried.*

*Then, for the first time in I can't remember when, the memory of Mama's gingerbread made me smile.*

Janet held Nora's story to her chest. It was so simple, so brief, yet so precious. *God, thank You for Kate's request of refreshments and help with her class. Thank You for sending me to Nora.*

She returned to the activities room, where she found Nora reading Ray's story with her white Good Shepherd pen poised for corrections. Janet tried not to giggle at the sight of Crosby sitting beside Harry's chair, in his funny dog sweater, staring up at Nora as if waiting for feedback on *his* story. Harry was at the next table over with Roberta, reading something while she looked on.

While waiting for Nora, Janet reached under the table for her tote bag and found a pen. She hunched over Nora's story and drew a big star at the top of it. She added a smiley face and the note, *Excellent! Your story made me cry for all the right reasons.*

She moved Nora's story to her place at the table and waited for her to come back. Then she remembered the cards in her pocket, grabbed the notepad, tucked the card she'd written to Nora under the story, and slid the notepad across the table again.

As soon as Nora sat down and picked up her story, Janet went over to her and wrapped her arms around her. She kissed Nora's cheek. She expected her to respond with a snarky comment. Instead, she leaned her head against Janet and said, "Thank you, Gingerbread Lady."

"Since I wrote all over the top of your story, I suggest we go to your room, get your laptop, and print a clean copy for Kate."

Class ended with such a long time of socializing and thanking Kate for her teaching that when Nora and Janet returned from printing the story, Nora asked, "We are still having one more class and a big celebration dinner next week, right?"

Roberta wrapped her arm around Nora's shoulders. "Yes, we are, but I'd say seeing everyone finish their stories is worth some extra celebration and time together."

Janet sneaked through the crowd and slipped a card into Kate's purse. Kate stopped her on her way back to her seat.

"Janet, can I ask a quick favor? After I get the last of the stories into the book document today, do you mind if I send it to you to look it over?"

Janet hesitated. After reading Nora's story, helping her print another copy, and walking in on the scene of Eileen, Ray, Harry, their friends from Good Shepherd, and new friends from the community smothering Kate with thanks, she wanted to say yes. Her to-do list for the celebration dinner, the café, and life in general told her otherwise. *How can I word this without upsetting what has been a wonderful morning?* "I'm sorry, Kate, but I don't think I can work it in."

"Not a problem. With all you're doing already, I completely understand." Kate squeezed Janet's arm. "There are other people I can ask."

The lack of pushback came as such a shock that Janet almost changed her mind. Before temptation got the best of her, she said, "I'm looking forward to the dinner. Debbie and I have a scrumptious menu planned."

"I can hardly wait. I so appreciate you hosting it. I feel like I've made some new friends."

"I do too." It felt strange but good to say that and mean it.

When she finished talking to Kate, everyone but Roberta and Harry had moved into the hallway to visit. Janet picked up her plate and dropped the cellophane into the trash can.

"Thanks again for showing me your story, Roberta," she heard Harry say. "I always felt like I let you down that day."

"You didn't let me down. We were both kids, and kids don't always make the brightest decisions."

Janet couldn't help stopping to interrupt on her way out the door. "Roberta, did I hear that you wrote a story for the anthology?"

"I sure did. Originally, it was just for Harry, but we talked, and I decided to add it to the anthology and have Kate place it right after his. Mine is titled 'Birdie's Confession.'"

Janet tucked her plate into her tote bag. "I wonder whatever happened to the man in the red cap."

"I was just telling Harry about that," Roberta said. "His name was Thomas Gray. I only know that because when the police caught up with him, they called me down to identify him. I told my parents and the police what really happened at the train station, but Thomas still ended up spending some time in jail for other crimes he had committed in the area."

"I imagine so." It still gave Janet chills to picture a grown man trying to yank away a little girl's camera for sneaking a picture. "No matter what you did, his reaction could have caused a lot more damage than it did."

"It didn't help that he also had multiple reports for loitering and theft against him. I've always hoped he got help and turned his life around."

Janet needed to get back to the café, but she had to ask Roberta one more question. "How did the fountain pen that Harry gave you end up in Uhrichsville?"

"I kept it with me until my husband passed and I started traveling a lot. I asked Maggie to hold on to a few things for safekeeping, including our old lap desk and my fountain pen. Maggie and her husband ended up in Uhrichsville when he retired from the ministry. Obviously, she kept her promise to take good care of the things from my childhood that she knew meant the most to me."

Kate joined the conversation. "I bet you had no idea that the pen was a collector's item."

"None at all. I kept it for the sentimental value."

Janet reached into her tote bag for her car key. "I'm even more sorry we lost it after hearing your story."

Roberta started collecting empty creamer cups and sweetening packets. "Who knows? Maybe it'll turn up."

# CHAPTER TWENTY-SEVEN

*C*oming." Janet plopped a peeled potato into the pot of water and dropped the peeler. She wove through the sea of pretty tablecloths to open the door of the café.

Kim stood in front of her with a box full of train memorabilia and more records, already wearing a classic black dress, green shimmery jacket, and simple silver jewelry, which matched the vintage theme. "I found a few more tunes for us in my collection." She glanced over her shoulder. "Look who I ran into in the parking lot just in time to solicit their help getting this stuff out of my car."

Behind her, Greg had Kim's record player and Jaxon and Julian each held one side of a table to use as a stand. All were clad in black slacks, white shirts, and bow ties.

Debbie set a tray of water glasses aside and pointed to the back corner of the café, farthest from the kitchen. "We have a spot ready for you right over there."

Greg walked past Debbie. "My tux jacket is in the car."

Jaxon and Julian followed their dad and said hello to Debbie and Janet.

Kim put her box on the counter. "This place looks incredible."

Janet plugged in the lights she'd strung around the writing station. "It's amazing what fancy tablecloths, lights, and candles can do to an ordinary railroad café."

Jaxon sniffed the air. "What are you cooking?"

Janet started unpacking the antique toy trains from Kim's box. "Our menu tonight includes a choice of roast beef or chicken served with mashed potatoes, roasted vegetable, and either apple crisp or chocolate cream pie for dessert."

"Did you do all the cooking?" Julian asked.

"Oh no. I'd like to think I could manage all that in addition to cooking for the café, but I had help. My friend Charla made the desserts and is assisting me in the kitchen tonight."

Kim took the small stack of records out of her box. "That settles it. My diet has officially been sabotaged. Not that it was going that well to begin with."

Debbie took the records from her. "I gave up on those long ago. Weight watching and working with my little pastry queen over here don't match."

Kim reached into her box again. "Before I take this box back to my office and touch up my makeup for the evening, I have a little something for the autograph portion of this little shindig." She took a wrapped package from the box and held it out to Janet.

"Kim." Janet took the package and carefully peeled the tape along the side. "What is this?"

"You'll see."

"Rip it," Julian called from the table where Greg was plugging in the record player.

Janet tore off the ribbon and paper and uncovered a calligraphy set that included three plastic fountain pens and ink in six different colors. "Oh, Kim. Thank you."

"I saw it on a post-holiday clearance shelf yesterday and couldn't resist. It may not replace the nice pen that you lost, but it will be a fun addition to the party."

Janet took the calligraphy set to the writing station. "What a perfect send-off for the message board." The board was so covered with artful words, quotes, verses, and pictures, she could no longer see the cork surface underneath. Even her own invitation to brighten someone's day in the dreary month of January was partially covered. In the center, Roberta's note to Harry still stood out with its elegant script.

Janet breathed a prayer. *Lord, the pen may have disappeared, but I'm thankful to at least know the story behind how it brought Harry and Roberta together.*

---

The Andrews Sisters played over the sound system just loudly enough to create a sense of fun. As each guest arrived, they commented on seeing their book displayed in Kim's ticket window. Now, everyone was getting seated for dinner. Greg offered Roberta his arm and ushered her to her reserved place at the same table as Kate, Nora, Anne, and Rick. Harry, Patricia, Ray, and Eileen were at the next table over. Janet put on her chef's hat and took a moment to watch Whistle Stop Café's first ever book-launch dinner. Each member of Kate's workshop had a spiral copy of *Our Collective Memory* from a local printer at their place, and Ian had volunteered to sell extra copies to guests at the register.

Back in the kitchen, Charla was putting the finishing touches on the meal. Janet picked up a basket of bread and a plate of butter pats shaped like roses and took them to Roberta's table.

"Good evening, Roberta." She set the bread and butter in the center of the table.

"Good evening, Janet." Roberta picked up her copy of *Our Collective Memory* and ran her hand over the cover featuring the old train station. "It doesn't matter how many times I look at this cover. I can't get over how nice it turned out."

Kate leaned over. "It's beyond what I expected for a spiral rush job."

Jaxon set a menu in front of Roberta. "May I get you something to drink?"

Roberta smiled at him. "Just water, thank you, young man."

Harry nudged Jaxon. "You and your brother clean up real nice."

"Thank you, Mr. Franklin."

Harry held up his copy of *Our Collective Memory* and opened it to the Table of Contents. "Look at this, Janet. All of us in this room are real writers now."

Janet read the list of familiar names—*Harry Franklin, Eileen Turner Palmer, Ray Zink, Nora Anderson, Roberta Daley*... "What are we going to do with all these famous people in one town?" She looked down at Crosby, who had a checked scarf tied around his neck and a new red dog sweater for the occasion. "Crosby, you let me know if Harry's head gets too big."

Patricia scooted her chair back. "I need to go buy my copy before Ian runs out. Excuse me a minute."

Kate waved Janet over. "Thank you so much for your card."

"You're welcome. I need to send cards more often."

"I will treasure yours forever." She got up from her chair. "Time to start the first part of the presentation."

Janet paused before she resumed serving bread and butter. She wanted to say a quick hello to Nora, who was stunning in a sparkly red dress.

"You look beautiful, Nora."

"Thank you." Nora patted her walker. It had curled gold and silver ribbon tied around each handle. "I even dressed my walker up for the occasion."

Janet laughed. "I love it."

"I figure it's not every day I get published."

Before Janet could respond, Kate tapped her water glass with her spoon.

"Everyone, may I have your attention?"

Janet gave Nora a gentle pat and found a spot close to the kitchen door so she'd be ready to serve dinner when the time came.

Paulette hurried to turn off the music.

Kate moved to the center of the room. "Before we eat, I want to thank all of you for coming. I especially want to thank Debbie Albright, Janet Shaw, and Charla Whipple for this incredible dinner. And to the anonymous benefactor who covered the cost of the dinner, I don't have enough words to express how grateful I am for your support of this event."

When the applause started, Janet gave a little curtsy and Debbie bowed, complete with a swoosh of her arm.

Charla came out of the kitchen and tipped her chef's hat. "Happy to be part of the fun."

"And to Kim Smith for graciously offering to sell copies of *Our Collective Memory* in the museum gift shop." She waved her hand at Anne. "As a special surprise, I have one more announcement. Thanks to Rick and Anne Peters, our book will also be for sale at Aunt Maggie's Antiques and Consignment."

Janet led the applause with a raucous, "Woo-hoo!"

"Now it's time to enjoy dinner. Then I will introduce you to our guest speaker."

Debbie inched over to Janet. "Did we set a place for the speaker?"

Janet glanced over at Kate's table. Every spot was full. "I set the number of places that Kate gave me a head count for."

"Could this person be coming after we eat?"

Janet headed for the kitchen. "I've never attended an event that had a speaker who only showed up for their talk."

Charla prepared two plates and handed them to Debbie then started on more for Jaxon, Julian, and Paulette. Janet followed Debbie out.

Debbie set one of her plates in front of Eileen and the other in front of Ray. Janet stopped at Kate's table. She leaned down behind her and whispered, "Where is the speaker?"

Kate shifted her body around. "She's here."

"Where? I know every person in this room."

Kate reached for her water glass. "Trust me. Our speaker is right here."

Janet stood up and looked at each face at each table, trying to guess who would be introduced as a local author.

# CHAPTER TWENTY-EIGHT

anet pushed the question of who the surprise speaker would be out of her mind in the dizzying fun of serving dinner and visiting with her guests. By the time she handed a tray of chocolate cream pie slices to Julian, and Charla passed another of apple crisps to Jaxon, she was too caught up in seeing Harry, Eileen, Ray, and the rest of the class enjoy themselves to think much about it.

She pushed the sectioned slicer into another chocolate pie. "We should do something like this again."

Paulette took a tray of desserts off the counter. "I agree. They're having a blast."

Roberta had moved to Harry and Patricia's table and had her pictures out. They were laughing hysterically over one of them.

Janet followed Paulette into the dining area. "I need to see what's going on over there."

She parked herself behind Roberta. "Excuse me, but you all are getting a bit too rowdy. I'm going to have to ask you to either leave or tell me what's so funny."

Patricia held up a blurry picture of Harry in his porter uniform at about age sixteen or seventeen. He was pushing a luggage cart into the depot and had his eyes half closed. His mouth hung open like he'd been caught midword.

Roberta set the baggie of pictures in front of Harry. "I snuck that of him when I was ten-going-on-eleven. I could be such a little brat."

Harry took another picture out of the bag. "But you were a cute little brat." He handed another snapshot to Janet. "Here's a good one."

She called Debbie over to look at the image of Harry taking a soldier's duffel bag off his hands. If Janet only had Harry and the soldier's expressions to go on, she would never guess that Birdie took the photo during a very long war. "Roberta, do you think it's possible to get copies of these pictures?"

"Already taken care of. Anne promised to scan them into her computer and make as many as I want. Kim requested some for the museum."

Once again, Kate tapped her water glass. "Everyone, I hate to interrupt your conversations, but while you enjoy your dessert, I would like to introduce our speaker."

Janet gave the picture back to Harry. "I'm going to check on our supply of decaf and hot water."

Debbie met Janet at the coffee station. "Watch, we'll find out that Kate is the speaker for her own event. Who else could it be?"

Janet clicked on the coffee maker. "It better not be me. I didn't prepare a speech." She turned so she could witness every detail of the big reveal.

Kate picked up a folder and opened it. "Our guest spent her childhood in Dennison and went on to write for a variety of newspapers, including thirty years with the *Cincinnati Times*. After retiring from journalism, she wrote about her international travels and began writing novels under the pen name Elsie James. Her novels have become bestsellers and won numerous awards."

Janet got a mental image of the novel by Elsie James that Debbie gave her for Christmas.

"Those of you who took my 'Tell Your Life Story' workshop will be thrilled to discover that you had a multi-published author in your midst, assisting you with your stories."

Harry glanced at Roberta.

Janet's mouth fell open.

"Though our speaker is no longer local, she told me she will always consider Dennison her hometown. Ladies and gentlemen, I am thrilled to introduce my dear friend, Roberta Daley."

When Roberta pushed her chair back and stood, Janet wished for a chair to collapse into from the exciting surprise of realizing she'd so recently had an impromptu tea with an author whose book lay on her coffee table at home.

Harry's face was frozen in such a big grin that Janet expected him to start a standing ovation.

Roberta took Kate's place in the center of the room. The commanding air that made her stand out whenever she entered the café was taken over by a humble, quieter confidence.

Harry continued clapping even after everyone else stopped. "Birdie? You did become a famous writer."

"Well, I don't know about famous. But the little girl who used to follow servicemen around at the Salvation Army canteen finally found a good use for her talents."

Janet pulled over chairs for herself and Debbie. "Now I'm sad that she lives in San Francisco. I like her more and more all the time."

Pride filled Harry's eyes. He exchanged smiles with Eileen. "That's our Birdie."

Eileen glanced from Harry to Roberta and back again. "I always had a feeling we would end up saying we knew her when."

Janet relaxed in her chair to take in Roberta's talk. She'd heard many authors speak during her mother's years of working for a publisher. Many of the talks she remembered focused on the author's most recent book or their writing journey. Roberta's felt different. She praised those who'd had the courage to sign up for Kate's workshop and tell their own stories, even when writing about the past was hard. When she finally did talk about herself, her stories of growing up in Dennison and becoming a regular fixture at the station came across as such fond memories that no one would know she was the girl who had a scary experience with a man who tried to yank her camera right off her body.

"I will never forget those days, and the kind friends who let me hang around and interview servicemen as if I knew what I was doing. I am especially grateful for a certain teenage porter named Harry."

All eyes turned to Harry. Janet saw him start to tear up and blew him a kiss.

"One night, I got myself into a bit of a scrape, and Harry and his friend Sylvia took care of me. They sat with me until my mother came to pick me up, and they asked to read my stories. They told me I was a good writer. Then Harry reached into his pocket and gave me what I know must have been a prized possession—his fountain pen. Harry, I want you to know that whenever the writing life got difficult—and that happened often—I thought about you giving me that pen. You were the first person who believed in me and called me talented. Nobody else asked to read my stories before that day.

My sister thought I was a pest. Kids at school thought I was weird, which I'm sure was true. My mother had so much on her plate that she didn't have time to read what I wrote in my composition book. But Harry took me seriously. He gave me a gift that made me feel like a writer. And because of that, I started thinking of myself as a real writer."

Kate reached behind her and squeezed Harry's shoulder.

Roberta walked back to her chair. "When Harry gave me his pen, neither of us had a clue that it would become a collector's item. A collector's item that my grand-niece, Anne, would sell to Janet Shaw for fifteen dollars. I could be really upset right now, knowing that special pen is gone. But I decided to see it as a reminder that sometimes we have no idea what we are giving away. Harry, the day you gave me your fountain pen, you gave me something far more valuable. You gave me confidence."

Roberta held her arms out to the entire group. "I want every one of you to know that you are good writers. I have loved every moment of listening to your stories and helping you get them into print. That book in the museum ticket window is just as valuable to me as an award-winning novel." She turned to Kate. "Now Kate and I want to give each of you a reminder that your stories are treasures to us and to your community."

Janet didn't realize how deeply Roberta's talk affected her until Debbie handed her a tissue and said, "And you got to be part of making this happen."

Janet leaned her head against Debbie's. "I'm so glad I did."

Kate reached under the table. She pulled out a box and set it on the table. The box had a huge red bow on the front and a scalloped-edge label that said *Writing Awards* in large block letters. "Each of your stories touched me in a unique way. So I want to honor every one of you with the Dennison Ohio Inspirational Author Award."

Debbie leaned toward Janet. "Did you know about this?"

Janet shook her head, unable to take her eyes off the award box. "No."

One by one, Kate called the names of those who participated in her workshop and said a little something about why she loved their writing while Roberta delivered their framed certificate.

"This is not the Kate I used to know at church," Debbie said.

Roberta handed Nora her award.

"Gran," Kate said, her voice tight with emotion, "yours was the story that made me cry the most. Thank you for letting me get to know you better."

Nora gave her a hug. Janet called out, "Yay, Nora!"

"And now…" Kate reached into the box. "I have one more award for the person who touched me with his enthusiasm and dedication to the workshop. Not only did he write two stories for the anthology, but one of those stories inspired a sequel. I'll let you all discover the two connected stories when you read the book. My Special Recognition Award goes to Harry Franklin."

Harry pointed to himself. "Me?"

"Yes, you," Janet shouted from across the room.

Nora boosted herself up with her walker to start a standing ovation for Harry.

Janet gave Kim a hug goodbye. "Thank you again for helping us make this event special."

"I wouldn't have missed it. Are you sure you don't want some help cleaning up?"

Debbie held the door open for her. "We're fine. Ian is coming back after helping with transportation to Good Shepherd. To make things easier, I think we'll keep the candles and fancy tablecloths out for tomorrow. They'll make for good conversation."

Janet sank into the chair across from Harry. She put her hands over her mouth and let out a squeal. "Oh my goodness, it's Harry Franklin, the award-winning author."

Roberta pushed her copy of *Our Collective Memory* across the table to him and pretended to weep into a napkin. "You are why I became a writer. I've read everything you've ever written. Will you please sign my book?"

Harry picked up one of the calligraphy pens that Kim provided. "Well, what do you know? I have my first groupies." He took Roberta's book from her but didn't open it. Instead, he set the calligraphy pen on top of it and folded his hands. "Before I give you my autograph, you have some explaining to do. How did you come up with Elsie James as a pen name? You insisted you would use Birdie L. Cummings."

"James was my late husband's name. I chose Elsie because of a talk I had with my sister Maggie about how much we disliked our names as kids. We thought they sounded like old ladies' names. As adults, we started using them as terms of affection. We ended every phone call with 'Love you, Margaret Constance. Love you too, Roberta Louise.'"

"Where did Elsie come in?"

"I decided it would be fun to combine the initials of our middle names. Originally, I was going to use L.C. James. Then I realized, wait, *Elsie*. L.C."

"Ah." Harry opened Roberta's book. "Now, that is clever."

Kate came to the table with Nora's coat over her arm. "Gran is getting tired. I'm going to take her back to Good Shepherd. Are you ready, Roberta?"

"As soon as I get my book signed."

Harry unscrewed the calligraphy pen. Janet got up to give Nora a goodbye hug. Before she had the chance to promise to visit her, Nora took hold of her wrist and looked deep into her eyes. The glow of party sparkle that lit her up during the dinner had faded to the same sad cloud that hovered over her the day she tried a bite of Janet's gingerbread.

Janet took her hand. "Are you okay, Nora?" Maybe she was just tired. Who could blame her?

Tears started collecting in Nora's eyes. "I need to tell you something."

Nora's voice was so quiet that Janet didn't know Harry and Kate heard her until they fell into a somber silence.

Harry pulled out the chair beside his. "Sit down, Nora. We're your friends. Talk to us."

Kate kept her hand on her grandmother's back until she'd lowered herself into the chair.

Janet sat on the other side of her. "What's wrong?"

Debbie locked the café door and joined them at the table.

Nora reached to take her purse from Kate. "Janet, I... I have something that belongs to you."

She unzipped her little black handbag and took out the copper-colored fountain pen. She set it in front of Janet.

"I'm sorry." She looked like a broken little girl. "I took it the day I came here with Kate."

Janet wanted to ask why. But all she could do was keep hold of Nora's hand.

Kate's mouth opened in shock. "You?" she finally managed.

"I didn't mean to. I..." She gripped Janet's hand harder. "My father used to own a fountain pen of that color. I saw it sitting there on the writing table, and I just wanted to hold it."

The expression on Roberta's face said she knew this confession was coming. She got up and put her hand on Nora's shoulder.

A week ago, Janet would have been angry. But after hearing Nora's stories and seeing the regret on her face, she realized how excruciating it must have been for her to spend the whole celebration dinner feeling miserable with guilt, and all she wanted to do was reassure her. She put her other hand over Nora's. "It's all right, Nora. How about if you just tell us what happened?"

Nora started to tremble. "When I came to the café with Kate that day, I saw the pen and thought of my dad's. He got the pen from his father when he finished medical school. He took it with him to Europe when he served in the medical corps. I remember Mama got upset because it wasn't with his belongings when the military sent them home. We figured it must have been lost."

Harry set Roberta's book aside. "Nora, did you come to the train station with your mom and brother to say goodbye to your daddy when you were a little girl?"

"Yes. I was six. It was right after Christmas. That was the only time Mama let us go with her to say goodbye to Daddy at the station. Every other time, we said goodbye at home."

"I remember you. You had a doll in your arms. Your dad tried to cheer you up by asking you to draw him a picture with your Christmas crayons." He touched Nora's arm. "Your daddy gave his fountain pen to me as a thank-you for returning his wallet after he dropped it. A few months later, I gave it to Roberta."

More tears spilled from Nora's eyes. "So it really is my father's?"

Harry nodded.

"I'm sorry for taking it, Janet. It's just that, when I picked it up, I felt close to my father again, like he was right there in the café standing beside me. So I put it in my pocket, to have it with me for a while longer." She loosened her grip on Janet's hands and wiped her tears. "Every time you sat listening to my stories and helping me decide what to write, I wanted to tell you what I did. When I went to my room to write the story about Mama's gingerbread, I set the pen next to my laptop, and the story flowed in one sitting." She gave Roberta a hesitant, sideways glance. "Roberta came in while I was writing. I put my notebook over it as quickly as I could. But I'm pretty sure she saw it. Why didn't you say anything?"

Roberta patted her shoulder and sat down. "I don't know. I wanted to. I guess I knew you'd do the right thing in time."

"I am truly sorry, Janet."

Janet picked up the fountain pen. At that moment, she cared more about Nora than the pen.

Nora looked at her pleadingly. "Are you going to call the police now?"

"No." Janet wanted to laugh but didn't have the heart to. "I'm not going to call the police over a pen. Even while I was searching for it, I knew deep down that I wouldn't press charges against the person who took it. I just wanted it back." She handed Nora a napkin. "Now I can give it to its rightful owner."

Nora wiped the last of her tears. "The question is, should the pen go to Harry, or Roberta?"

# CHAPTER TWENTY-NINE

Roberta looked across the table at Harry. "If you don't mind, Janet, I think the pen should go to Harry. I had it for a long time. Now it's time for him to have it back."

Harry shook his head. "That's kind of you, Roberta, but I wouldn't feel right taking it."

"But I want you to have it."

Janet got up from the table and set the pen in front of Harry. "Before it went missing, I planned to give it to you anyway. Along with the picture little Tabatha drew after you let her try it out."

Harry picked up the pen. "Using this pen did bring back good memories, even when I thought it only looked like the one I used to have. But the rightful owner isn't me." He got up and held the pen out to Nora. "This belonged to your father. Now it belongs to you."

"It wouldn't be right." Nora pointed to the writing station. "I stole it from that table."

Janet took the pen from Harry, placed it in Nora's palm, and closed her fingers over it. "I think it's safe to say that every person in this room wants you to have this."

Kate put her arm around her grandmother. "Please accept it, Gran. I remember you telling me you didn't have anything of value that belonged to your parents. Now you'll have something."

Nora held the pen to her heart. She smiled in a way that Janet didn't know she was capable of. "Are you sure?"

Harry sat back down at his place. "One hundred percent."

"Thank you. You're a good man."

Janet remembered the spare bottle of ink that Anne gave her when she bought the desk and pen. "I'll bring you some refill ink tomorrow." Noticing how teary everyone at the table was, she suggested, "Now, how about if I get us some proper tissue out of my purse so we can stop using napkins?"

Debbie ran her fingertips under her eyelids. "I know I could use one."

Janet hurried to the kitchen, where she'd stashed her purse. When she returned to the table, Harry was walking Nora over to the writing station while Crosby waited at the table with Debbie. Janet stood and watched Harry pull out the chair for Nora and hold the back of it while she sat. They seemed set apart in their own world. Harry took down the note that Nora had written the first time she came into the café and handed it to her. Then he left her alone and came to stand with Janet.

After handing the packet of tissues to Debbie, Janet wrapped her arms around Harry's shoulders. "What you did was so kind."

"We all need something to remember those we love. From what I observed between the two of you in class, you were pretty kind yourself."

Kate went to help her grandmother pin her note back up on the board.

"What did you write, Nora?" Harry asked on his way over to the desk.

Nora capped her fountain pen. "I corrected my note."

Janet went over to read it. "Now I'm curious too." Once Harry stepped aside, she took her turn.

*Make the most of today.*
*You never know what life might throw at you tomorrow...*
*And you don't want to miss God's surprises.*

"That's beautiful, Nora." Janet ran her fingers over the etchings on the side of the lap desk. "Now you'll have a lovely pen for writing more stories about your life."

Kate took the tissue pack from Debbie. "And to write letters to Janet, Harry, and Roberta."

Debbie brought over a trash can for everyone to toss tissues into. "She won't need to write to them if she's at Good Shepherd. Janet and I go there all the time to visit Eileen and Ray."

Nora put the fountain pen in her purse. "I guess this is as good a time as any to share our good news." She reached for Kate's hand. "I'm not staying at Good Shepherd after all. Kate and I are going to be roomies."

Janet got up to clear dishes off the other tables. "Where will you live?"

Nora let go of Kate's hand. "My house in Barnhill. My son might be ready for me to sell it, but I'm not."

Kate picked up her purse. "My house is in foreclosure, and I'm going through a divorce. Gran and I talked, and I decided it would be good for me to leave Cleveland for a fresh start. Gran said I can live with her."

Nora stood up. "It's what family does. They take care of each other."

Janet handed a stack of plates to Debbie. "I hope you stop by the café often."

Crosby laid his head on Harry's knee, and Harry stroked his ears. "Hey, Kate, maybe you can teach another workshop, now that you're going to be a local."

Kate put on her coat. "Maybe I will. Who knows?"

Harry rubbed Crosby's back. "If you do, I'll be the first to sign up. I'm on a roll with writing stories."

Nora looked up at all the notes. "So what are you going to do with your message board now that January is over?"

Janet tried to picture that spot without the writing station. It would seem so blank and boring. "Maybe we can take it out again once in a while."

Kate picked up the empty box that held the awards. "May I suggest one thing? If you do this again and decide to include a pen, use the pens Kim gave you."

Janet picked up one of the calligraphy pens and examined it like Kim would study something of great historic significance. "But are you *sure* these are cheapies and not vintage?"

"I'm sure. I have some like them at home. They came in plastic packaging."

Harry reached for Roberta's copy of *Our Collective Memory.* "I'll take one of those cheapie pens. I still have a book to sign."

Roberta sat back down. "You can autograph it, 'To my lifelong friend, Roberta.'"

"I'm glad we're on the same page." Harry flipped to the Table of Contents and put stars beside his story titles. "I was about to write something to that effect."

He turned to the title page.

Nora stuck her fountain pen between Harry's face and the book. "Use our pen. It's better."

Roberta reached into her purse and took out the notebook that Janet saw her writing in the day before the fountain pen disappeared.

Janet sucked in her breath. *She's a writer. Writers take notes. That explains her behavior on the day Kim was here.* Still, she had to ask, "What are you writing over there?"

Roberta took out a pen and clicked it. "Notes for my next book. Ever since I walked into this place, my brain has been buzzing with ideas."

Dear Reader,

Back in the days when my two sons and I regularly rode Amtrak's California Zephyr between Reno, Nevada, and California's San Francisco Bay Area, I never dreamed I would someday be writing for a mystery series based at a historic train station. Yet here I am doing just that and having a blast. I consider it such an honor to be part of the Whistle Stop Café Mystery team.

Like many writers, I have a strange attraction to office supplies, especially pens. One of my absolute favorite writing instruments is a fountain pen. Since I can't afford the high-end pens that I have admired so often in stationery stores and on calligraphy blogs, I decided to write a story that included one and give it to a dear Whistle Stop Café regular—Harry Franklin. I underestimated how fun it would be to give Harry a voice and a history that included working as a porter at Dennison Station as a teenager, making a difference in the lives of others and first meeting his late wife, Sylvia.

The process of writing this book reminded me of the power of encouragement and the importance of recording our personal stories, both for ourselves and those who come after us. Each of us has something valuable to share with the world, whether it is published or not.

Thank you to Guideposts Books and Susan Downs for allowing me to be part of your family of authors. And thank you to each person who picks up this book. May God bless you as you live the adventure that He has you on.

Signed,
Jeanette Hanscome

# ABOUT the AUTHOR

Jeanette Hanscome is a multi-published author of both fiction and nonfiction, and a big fan of train travel.

When she isn't writing, Jeanette gravitates toward all things creative, especially now that her two sons are grown. After decades of singing without the ability to accompany herself, she took up ukulele during the pandemic with the help of YouTube videos. Experimenting with a variety of styles—including Celtic songs and music originally written for the lute (because, why not?)—is one of her favorite ways to relax after a day of writing. Jeanette writes and plays from her bedroom/office in the San Francisco Bay Area.

# A GLIMPSE *of the* PAST

We are all familiar with the picture of Rosie the Riveter flexing her bicep—a representation of the countless women who kept factories, defense plants, shipyards, and railroads running during WWII while the men fought overseas. One detail that slipped through the cracks of history (until recently) was the recognition of the more than a half-million "Black Rosies" who worked tirelessly for the war effort alongside their white counterparts.

Women like Sylvia and her aunt Marion faced racism and harassment, often while doing dangerous work. But for many, it was a chance to exchange demeaning work as domestics and sharecroppers for jobs they could take pride in. For the first time, they felt empowered and made more money. Best of all, they experienced the satisfaction of doing their part. Black Rosies became shipbuilders, electricians, welders, and train conductors.

These women and their remarkable contribution to World War II went unnoticed until African American historians and writers shed light on them. I couldn't think of a better match for Harry Franklin than a determined, confident young woman who had no idea she was making history while working as a mechanic.

# FROM the HOME-FRONT KITCHEN

## Janet's Gingerbread
### Makes 2 loaves

**Ingredients:**

1 cup brown sugar

½ cup butter, softened

¾ to 1 cup molasses (Janet used just under a cup)

¼ cup pure maple syrup

1 teaspoon vanilla

2 teaspoons baking soda

1 cup boiling water

3 cups all-purpose flour

1 teaspoon each cinnamon, ginger, nutmeg, allspice, and ground clove

½ teaspoon salt

2 eggs, beaten

Powdered sugar for dusting

**Directions:**

Preheat oven to 350 degrees.

Grease two loaf pans.

Blend sugar and butter in medium bowl. Add molasses, maple syrup, and vanilla.

Measure 1 cup boiling water in 2-cup measuring cup. Add baking soda and stir well.

Sift flour and spices into large bowl. Add salt, molasses mixture, and baking soda water. Stir well. Add eggs and stir again.

Pour into greased loaf pans. Bake for about 45 minutes or until cake tester comes out clean.

Before serving, dust with powdered sugar.

Top with whipped cream, drizzled icing, or your favorite topping.

*Read on for a sneak peek of another exciting book
in the Whistle Stop Café Mysteries series!*

# FOR SENTIMENTAL REASONS

### BY GABRIELLE MEYER

*A* cold wind rattled the windows on Debbie Albright's house as she pulled the pan of lasagna from her oven. The smell of basil and garlic wafted through her kitchen and made her stomach rumble. February in Ohio made her crave comfort foods, like pasta and soups, and she had spent much of the winter cooking some of her favorites. Since she lived alone, she knew she'd be eating lasagna for a few days. A thought that didn't bother her in the least.

The front doorbell rang, surprising her. She wasn't expecting anyone, although, since returning to her hometown of Dennison, she often had family and friends drop in.

She smiled to herself as she walked through her living room to the foyer. Things had changed since leaving her corporate job in Cleveland to come back to Dennison and open the Whistle Stop Café. She just wished she had made the move sooner. She loved impromptu visitors.

Debbie flipped on her front light and was surprised to see her aunt Sherry, her dad's sister. Aunt Sherry was almost eighty and didn't often go out in the evenings, especially during this time of year—and rarely by herself. In recent years, she'd been traveling to Arizona for the colder months. But this winter she had decided to stay in Dennison to get her house ready to sell. She planned to make a permanent move.

Debbie opened the door, allowing a gust of frosty air to blow past her.

"Come in," she said as she motioned for her aunt to enter. "It's cold out there."

Aunt Sherry held an old crate in her hands, making Debbie even more curious about her unexpected arrival.

"Hello, dear," Aunt Sherry said. "I hope I'm not bothering you."

"Of course not. I was just ready to sit down to eat supper. Would you like to join me?"

"Oh, I couldn't." Aunt Sherry wore a fur cap over her short gray hair. "I wouldn't want to bother you."

"You're no bother—and I have a whole pan of lasagna for myself. I'd love to share it."

"Well." Aunt Sherry glanced toward the kitchen and smiled. "I was just going to have a bowl of cereal when I got home."

"Then it's settled." Debbie took the crate from her aunt, surprised to see it filled with old baby items and a yellowed newspaper. "You're staying."

"It smells delicious." Aunt Sherry took off her heavy coat and her hat and set them on a hook.

"What did you bring for me?" Debbie asked as she indicated the crate.

Aunt Sherry's smile fell, and she shook her head. "I don't know what this is—that's why I brought it to you. I found it in the garage rafters today—or, I should say that my neighbor boy found it. I hired him to clean out the garage. You know I'm hoping to put my house up for sale soon, so I started going through things. And I found this crate."

Aunt Sherry had purchased her parents' house and had raised her two children there. Both of her kids had moved out of the area when Debbie was a little girl. Her husband had died a few years ago, and Aunt Sherry lived on her own.

"Let's take it into the living room," Debbie suggested. "The lasagna needs a few minutes to set before we cut into it."

Aunt Sherry followed Debbie, and they took a seat on the couch.

The crate was old and dusty. Cobwebs filled the corners, and the items within looked like they were in rough shape. There was a moth-eaten baby blanket, gray with age, though it must have been a soft pink at one time. There was also a silver rattle, a glass baby bottle, and a yellowed cotton sleeping gown.

"This is why I brought this stuff to you," Aunt Sherry said as she lifted the newspaper out of the crate. She carefully unfolded it and laid it on the coffee table.

"Look at the date," she said. "February fifteenth, 1944."

It was the Dennison newspaper, *The Evening Chronicle*. Right under the title of the paper was the biggest headline of the day. ALLIES ATTACK DURING STORM AND SHOVE GERMANS BACK IN BATTLE TO SAVE BEACHHEAD.

"This is interesting," Debbie said slowly. She didn't know why her aunt had brought it to her.

"Look at this." Aunt Sherry pointed to a smaller headline.

The ink was faded, so Debbie had to get closer to read it, but when she did, things started to make sense. "'Abandoned Baby Found at Dennison Depot by Depot Workers.'" Debbie went on to read the rest of the article out loud.

"'A baby girl was found yesterday, February fourteenth, abandoned on the platform of the Dennison depot. The porter heard the baby crying after the last train pulled out, and located the child. It is believed the baby is only a few days old. She was in a wooden crate with nothing more than a pink blanket, a small silver rattle, an empty baby bottle, and the white cotton gown she wore. The police were called, and the baby was placed in the care of a Dennison family until the mother can be located. Please contact the Dennison Police Department if you have any information on the identity of the mother or if you saw anything suspicious at the depot yesterday.'"

Debbie met her aunt's concerned gaze.

"I thought," Aunt Sherry said, "that since you and Janet work at the depot and you've solved so many mysteries there, that you might be able to help me solve this one."

Debbie and her best friend, Janet Shaw, had opened the Whistle Stop Café at the depot the past summer, and Debbie had shared many stories with her aunt about the mysteries they had solved. She wasn't surprised that her aunt would think of her now.

"Have you heard about this baby before?" Aunt Sherry asked, her blue eyes searching Debbie's with an intensity that surprised her.

"I haven't. I'm sorry. But I can see what Kim might know." Kim Smith was the director of the train museum, which was also housed in the depot. "I can ask some of my friends who worked at the depot and the Salvation Army canteen during the war. They might remember."

Aunt Sherry nodded and then gazed down at her hands.

"What's bothering you?" Debbie asked, putting her hand on her aunt's shoulder.

When Aunt Sherry finally looked up, she had tears in her eyes. "I was born on Valentine's Day in 1944, Debbie. My parents had been married for a decade before I came along—and then it was many years after that before they had your father. He was a complete surprise. I remember when my mom got pregnant with Vance. I was twelve— almost thirteen—and it was the shock of her life. I vividly recall her saying, 'I never thought it was possible.'" Aunt Sherry shook her head. "At the time, I thought she said it because she was in her forties. But now, after finding this crate hidden in the garage and seeing the date on the newspaper, I can't help but wonder if she said it because she didn't think she could *ever* get pregnant. What if I'm the baby who was abandoned on the depot platform that day?"

Debbie stared at her aunt, speechless. She had never been led to believe that Aunt Sherry was adopted—but it was entirely possible. Debbie had inherited her father's brown eyes, and she'd been told that both of his parents had brown eyes. Yet Aunt Sherry had blue eyes. She was also taller than all the other women in her family and didn't look a thing like Debbie's father. Yet Debbie had never questioned any of this.

Until now.

"I'll be eighty years old two weeks from yesterday," Aunt Sherry continued, tears streaking down her wrinkled cheeks. "And suddenly my entire life feels like a lie."

Debbie reached out and took Aunt Sherry's hand in her own. "Even if it's true, your life is not a lie. You are Sherry Albright Hoffman. Your parents were Fred and Gertrude Albright, and your brother is Vance. You have led a happy, fulfilled life, and you have two wonderful children. None of that is a lie, Aunt Sherry."

"Why wouldn't my parents tell me the truth?" she asked.

"We don't even know if you are the baby from the depot."

"How will we find out?"

"We can look for some answers," Debbie said with confidence. "We'll first find out if the baby or her mother was ever identified. Perhaps she was returned to her mother. If nothing comes of that, and we still want to know, we can always have a DNA test done to see if you're related to my dad—or me."

"I don't think I'm quite ready for that yet. That's why I'd like you to find out what you can first. Because why would my parents have the crate and other things from this baby if it wasn't me?"

"I don't know. There has to be some good explanation. Maybe your parents were the ones who took care of the baby until she could be reunited with her mother, and they just never got around to getting these things to her." Debbie squeezed her aunt's hand. "There's always a logical reason. We just have to find it."

Aunt Sherry was quiet for a moment, and then she said, "If this is me—if I was the baby abandoned, I want to know who my birth mother is and why she left me on the depot platform."

Debbie studied her aunt. "Would you really want to know?"

"Yes." Aunt Sherry lifted her chin. "I'm almost eighty years old. I want to know for my children's and grandchildren's sake if nothing else. They should know their heritage."

"It's all conjecture at this point," Debbie said. "We don't even know if it's you. We'll cross that bridge when we get to it."

"Okay." Aunt Sherry wiped at her tears.

"Now," Debbie said as she stood, "how about we dig into that lasagna? It should be set and ready to eat."

"That sounds wonderful." Aunt Sherry smiled at Debbie. "And thanks for helping me."

"Of course. We'll find the answers, Aunt Sherry. Don't worry."

Debbie led Aunt Sherry into her kitchen, her mind churning with all the questions her aunt's discovery had created.

⁂

The morning sun had not yet peeked above the horizon the next day as Debbie left her house to go to the Whistle Stop Café. Janet did all the baking and arrived between four and five, but Debbie usually got there at six to open for their early-morning customers.

It was only a few blocks from Debbie's house to the depot where the café was located, and she often walked. But during the winter, when there was ice and snow on the ground, she almost always drove to work. Not only was it nice to have a warm vehicle, but it was also nice to have her car at work in case she needed to run errands after they closed the café.

This morning, Debbie was especially anxious to get to work to talk to Janet about what Aunt Sherry had found. Aunt Sherry had left the crate with Debbie, and Debbie had brought it with her to the café to show Janet.

She pulled up to the depot and parked her car. The air was brisk as she got out and grabbed the crate. It wasn't very big, and it was almost hard to imagine a newborn fitting inside. How desperate that mama must have felt to leave her baby on the depot platform, and how cold and alone the baby must have been. If the weather was anything like it was today, and all the baby had for protection was a blanket, it was a miracle it hadn't frozen to death.

Debbie had so many questions as she walked into the depot. They had been spinning in her mind since her aunt's visit and had caused her to dream some strange dreams. Who found the baby? Was the mother ever identified? Why did the mother abandon the baby? Did the birth father know? What happened to the baby?

Most importantly, *was* Aunt Sherry the baby?

Debbie unlocked the main doors of the depot and turned left. She flipped on a few lights and then walked through the original waiting area and past the ticket counter to get to the glass door that led into the café. That door was locked as well, since Janet usually entered the kitchen through the back door and left the main doors locked until Debbie arrived.

The café bell above the door jangled, welcoming Debbie to another day of work.

She loved the café. Loved being her own boss and working alongside her childhood friend. She especially loved the customers that came in every day. These were the regulars, but then there were visitors who came to Dennison to visit the museum or stay in the bed-and-breakfast train car behind the depot.

No matter why they came, Debbie relished being in the front of the café to visit and get to know people. Janet enjoyed that too, but she also loved being in the kitchen. They were a perfect team.

Only one light was on above the register, so Debbie turned the rest of them on and then walked across the room to set the crate on the long counter. Swivel stools lined the counter, while tables and chairs filled the rest of the room. Bright yellow walls were covered with vintage WWII posters that Debbie and Janet had collected, as well as old kitchen utensils and tools that Janet had been given by her old employer. Behind the counter was a large chalkboard where they wrote the daily specials. Janet had already made the change from yesterday and had written *Meat loaf, mashed potatoes, gravy, and glazed carrots* for today's special.

Janet walked through the swinging door, pushing it open with her backside and bringing with her a sweet aroma. In her hands was a huge tray of caramel rolls, probably fresh out of the oven. Gooey, golden goodness oozed between the cracks and down the sides of the rolls.

"*Mm*," Debbie said, her stomach rumbling. "Those smell delicious."

"Hey." Janet smiled as she set the tray on the counter and opened the display case. She wore a pair of blue jeans and a graphic T-shirt, though Debbie couldn't read the words because her apron covered it.

"Good morning." Debbie slipped her coat off and hung it on the hook near the kitchen door. She took her apron from the hook next to it, put it on, and tied the strings.

"What's this?" Janet asked as she wiped her hands on her apron and nodded at the crate.

Debbie walked to the counter, adjusting her apron to fit over her blouse and blue jeans. "My aunt Sherry brought this crate to me last night."

"It looks old."

"The newspaper is from February fifteenth, 1944."

Janet lifted her eyebrows. Her chin-length blond hair was tucked behind her ears, and her hazel eyes were filled with curiosity. "What's up with the baby stuff?"

"Read the article at the bottom of the front page."

As Janet pulled the paper out and started reading the article, Debbie walked behind the counter and grabbed a plate and a mug. The smell of coffee already permeated the air, since Janet often started the first pot when she came in. Debbie filled her mug and helped herself to one of the caramel rolls.

"Wow," Janet said. "I've never heard about this. Have you?"

"No." Debbie took a seat on one of the stools and sipped the coffee, savoring the flavor and warmth. "But my aunt is concerned. She was born on February fourteenth, 1944, and she found the crate and the items inside the garage that used to belong to her parents. She thinks she might be the baby."

Janet frowned. "Did her parents ever say anything about adopting her?"

"Never." Debbie realized she had forgotten a fork, but Janet came to her rescue and handed her one. "Thanks."

Debbie cut into the caramel roll. It was so soft and moist, her mouth started to water even before she tasted it. "My grandparents were married for over ten years before my aunt was born, and then they didn't have my dad for another thirteen years. Aunt Sherry said that her mother claimed she never thought it was possible to get pregnant when she found out she was having Dad."

"Well, that's strange."

"I thought the same thing. My aunt is pretty shaken up about it." Debbie took the first bite, and it practically melted in her mouth. "This is really good, Janet."

"Thanks." Janet smiled, but then she nodded at the crate. "What do you think? Is it possible your aunt is the baby who was abandoned on the depot platform?"

"I don't know, but I can't rule it out."

"I wonder if Eileen remembers what happened."

"That's what I was wondering too."

Eileen Palmer had been the stationmaster at the Dennison depot during the war years, when the Salvation Army canteen served over a million soldiers as they came through town. She now lived at the Good Shepherd Retirement Center and had a wealth of knowledge about the town. She was also Kim Smith's mother.

"Kim might know something too," Janet said. "We should ask her."

Debbie nodded. "Are you free to run out to Good Shepherd with me after we close? I'll call Eileen and see if she's able to visit with us."

"I think that should work."

"Great."

A timer went off in the kitchen. "Those are my cranberry muffins," Janet said, and hurried off.

Debbie quickly finished her caramel roll as the first customer, Patricia Franklin, entered the café.

"Morning," Debbie said to Patricia.

"Good morning." Patricia shivered and then said, "Brr. It's cold out there today."

"I'm ready for a warm-up."

"Me too."

"The usual?"

"You know it."

Debbie took another sip of coffee and picked up her dirty plate to put it in the bin under the counter. She kept her coffee close at hand as she made a peppermint mocha for Patricia. "Janet has some fresh caramel rolls—"

"No need to convince me." Patricia grinned as she came over to the counter. "Sounds wonderful."

The day had begun, and Debbie was off and running, but she couldn't stop thinking about her aunt Sherry or the crate of baby items. As soon as she finished making Patricia's coffee, she lifted the crate off the counter and set it in the back, near the door that led outside.

More than anything, she hoped her aunt would get an answer that made her happy. But if she didn't, Debbie prayed that they could identify the birth mother and get the answers they needed.

# A NOTE FROM the EDITORS

We hope you enjoyed another exciting volume in the Whistle Stop Café Mysteries series, published by Guideposts. For over seventy-five years, Guideposts, a nonprofit organization, has been driven by a vision of a world filled with hope. We aspire to be the voice of a trusted friend, a friend who makes you feel more hopeful and connected.

By making a purchase from Guideposts, you join our community in touching millions of lives, inspiring them to believe that all things are possible through faith, hope, and prayer. Your continued support allows us to provide uplifting resources to those in need. Whether through our communities, websites, apps, or publications, we inspire our audiences, bring them together, and comfort, uplift, entertain, and guide them. Visit us at guideposts.org to learn more.

We would love to hear from you. Write us at Guideposts, P.O. Box 5815, Harlan, Iowa 51593 or call us at (800) 932-2145. Did you love *Accentuate the Positive*? Leave a review for this product on guideposts.org/shop. Your feedback helps others in our community find relevant products.

*Find inspiration, find faith, find Guideposts.*

Shop our best sellers and favorites at
## guideposts.org/shop

Or scan the QR code to go directly to our Shop